The
Sentence of the Court
A Handbook for Magistrates

A basic outline of the law and practice of sentencing in magistrates' courts, produced under the auspices of the Justices' Clerks' Society for use by newly appointed justices of the peace and other people concerned with the sentencing of offenders in summary proceedings.

The
Sentence of the Court
A Handbook for Magistrates

Published 1995 by
WATERSIDE PRESS
Domum Road
Winchester SO23 9NN
Telephone or Fax 01962 855567

ISBN Paperback 1 872 870 25 2

Cataloguing-in-Publication Data A catalogue record for this book can be obtained from the British Library

Printing and binding Antony Rowe Ltd, Chippenham

Cover design John Good Holbrook Ltd, Coventry

The

Sentence of the Court
A Handbook for Magistrates

Michael Watkins
Winston Gordon
Anthony Jeffries

Foreword by

Lord Taylor of Gosforth
Lord Chief Justice

Consultant Dr David Thomas

Editor Bryan Gibson

WATERSIDE PRESS
WINCHESTER

The authors

Michael Watkins is Director of Legal Services and Joint Justices' Clerk for Warwickshire. He has contributed to training programmes for magistrates at the Universities of Birmingham and Cambridge and is a member of the Executive Committee of the Justices' Clerks' Society Standing Committee of Magistrates' Training Officers. He is a solicitor and a member of the Society's Criminal Law Network.

Winston Gordon is Justices' Clerk and Training Officer for Tameside, Greater Manchester, a member of the Executive Committee of the Justices' Clerks' Society Standing Committee of Magistrates' Training Officers and chairs the Duchy of Lancaster Branch Training Committee. He is a solicitor—with experience of prosecuting and defending in the magistrates' court—and a member of the Society's Criminal Law Network.

Anthony Jeffries is Justices' Chief Executive and Justices' Clerk for Birmingham and Sutton Coldfield and a member of the Executive Committee of the Justices' Clerks' Society Standing Committee of Magistrates' Training Officers. He is a barrister and a member of the Advisory Group for Magistrates' Courses, Board of Continuing Education, University of Cambridge.

Consultant

Dr David Thomas is a barrister and Reader in Criminal Justice, University of Cambridge. He is a fellow of Trinity Hall, Cambridge, Editor of *Current Sentencing Practice*, Sentencing Editor of *Archbold* and Sentencing Cases Editor of the *Criminal Law Review* (all published by Sweet and Maxwell).

Editor

Bryan Gibson is Managing Editor of Waterside Press.

The
Sentence of the Court
A Handbook for Magistrates

Contents

Note The handbook deals with *adult* offenders, ie those aged 18 years and over. Younger offenders normally appear in the youth court where they are sentenced by specially trained magistrates. Exceptionally, offenders below the age of 18 may be sentenced in the ordinary magistrates' court (eg when the case also involves an adult). The handbook deals with the sentencing of people under 18 years of age only to this extent: see *Appendix E.*

Foreword

by The Right Honourable Lord Taylor of Gosforth

Lord Chief Justice

The process of sentencing a convicted defendant is one of the most important duties of any judge or magistrate. There is, of course, an ever-growing body of statute and case-law which sets out which punishments are available in which circumstances, and which criteria should serve as guidance. Much has also been written by academics, practising lawyers, journalists and politicians on the subject. But, in the courtroom, the decision of what sentence within those which the law allows is to be imposed on a particular offender for a particular crime is exclusively a matter for the discretion of the judicial officer before whom the case has been conducted.

This handbook, produced by Justices' Clerks and with the assistance of one of the country's foremost experts on sentencing, is intended to help magistrates by bringing together in one manageable volume a number of the most important statutory provisions and authorities within the overall framework established by Parliament. I hope it will be of use to Justices throughout the country as they consider how best to exercise the responsibilities society has vested in them.

Aims and Objectives

This handbook was compiled under the auspices of the Justices' Clerks' Society by three experienced training officers to magistrates. The aims were:

• to provide a companion for new magistrates as they undertake their basic training and come new to the task of sentencing

• to assist trainers by allowing them to concentrate on imparting skills necessary for making informed, balanced and structured sentence decisions—in the knowledge that background material can be found in the handbook

• to provide an accessible reference point for magistrates generally

• to inform other court users and students about how sentence decisions are approached in magistrates' courts; and

• to produce a lucid account, avoiding jargon and complexity. Statutory and other references—the province of court legal advisors and other lawyers—are not reproduced unless particularly significant or where they are in common, everyday use. *The handbook cannot replace legal advice, which should be sought in all but the most straightforward cases.*

Chapter 1

Introduction

Virtually all criminal prosecutions—ranging from those for the simplest parking offences to the most heinous murders—start out in the magistrates' court. Around 97 per cent are dealt with to their final conclusion by magistrates, either by acquittal or conviction and sentence. Conviction stems from a plea of 'guilty' or from a finding of guilt—based on the evidence in the case—where someone has pleaded 'not guilty'. Over 1.3 million cases a year are sentenced by magistrates. The remaining cases are dealt with by the Crown Court, having been sent there by magistrates' courts: for trial by jury; for sentence; or to be dealt with: see *Chapter 2*.

JURISDICTION

The sentencing powers of magistrates are laid down by Act of Parliament. Jurisdiction to deal with cases and, in many instances, the maximum sentence available depends on the status of the offence. There are two main classifications (the first of which is divided into two sub-categories):

Indictable offences

(i) Indictable only
Purely indictable offences can only be dealt with by the Crown Court. Examples are: murder (which carries a mandatory life-sentence), rape, robbery, serious firearms offences, serious drugs offences and wounding with intent to do grievous bodily harm. These offences are brought before a magistrates' court initially, but must then be sent to the Crown Court for trial before a judge and jury.

(ii) Either way offences
Either way offences can be tried by magistrates (ie 'summarily') or by the Crown Court (ie 'on indictment'). The decision as to venue is arrived at via a procedure known as 'mode of trial': *Chapter 2*. Common examples are: theft, criminal damage, assault occasioning actual bodily harm, lesser drugs offences and burglary (provided that this last offence

is not 'aggravated', eg involving the use of a weapon—when it becomes indictable only).

Where either way cases *are* heard by magistrates their sentencing powers are limited to six months imprisonment and/or a fine of £5,000 per offence—plus any ancillary orders (such as compensation or disqualification) which are appropriate. Sentences of imprisonment may be made concurrent to one another, or consecutive: see *Chapter 3*. Where consecutive sentences are passed by magistrates for two or more either way offences their maximum powers are 12 months in aggregate.

The Crown Court always has power to pass a longer sentence for an either way offence than the magistrates' court does (eg theft: up to seven years; criminal damage: up to ten years). Where an offender has been convicted by a magistrates' court following their decision that the case is more suitable for summary trial, there is power to commit for sentence if the magistrates later consider that the greater sentencing powers of the Crown Court should be invoked: *Chapter 2*.

Summary offences
In the normal course of events, summary offences can only be tried and sentences for them can only be passed by a magistrates' court. Examples of purely summary offences are: most road traffic offences (*Chapter 7*), the less serious public order offences, having 'no television licence' and contravening local bye-laws. The magistrates deal with the entire case: taking a plea, deciding upon guilt or innocence and—in the event of conviction—the sentence. Only in limited circumstances can summary offences be sent to the Crown Court for trial or sentence (eg where the summary matter is interwoven with more serious matters).

The maximum sentence for a summary offence is fixed by the statute which creates the offence, usually by reference to one of five fining levels (*Chapter 3*) or in some instances imprisonment of one, two, three or six months.

BACKGROUND TO CURRENT PRACTICE

The Criminal Justice Act 1991 made significant changes to the way in which the sentencing of offenders is approached. The criteria set out in that Act serve as a framework for present day sentencing practice. An underlying aim was to ensure that sentences are proportionate to the seriousness of the offence or offences of which an offender stands convicted. The 1991 Act uses the term 'commensurate' to describe such sentences—and at the time of the legislation the government called this a 'just deserts' approach. Principal features of the Act (which was amended in 1993 and 1994) are:

A framework for sentencing

A legal framework was created within which there are statutory criteria for the use of fines, community sentences and custody. In effect, the facts of a case—ie information about the offence—must be considered alongside these criteria. The framework is explained in *Chapter 3* of this handbook, which identifies four levels of sentence as follows:

- discharges
- fines
- community sentences; and
- custody.

When passing sentence, a court must decide upon

- the appropriate level of sentence within the framework; and
- the extent of the chosen sentence (eg the *size* of a fine, the total *number of hours* community service, the *length* of a prison sentence).

Seriousness

The 1991 Act made the seriousness of the offence the principal focus of sentence decision-making. Assessing seriousness involves:

- forming a view about the general level of seriousness of an offence. In order to bring about consistency of approach, each bench has its own local guidelines, or it may follow the Magistrates' Association *Sentencing Guidelines* (see *Appendix B* to this handbook) or a variant of these;

- then looking at the facts of the individual offence and considering aggravating factors (ie which make the offence more serious than other offences of its type) and mitigating factors (which make it less so). Examples of seriousness factors are contained in *Chapter 2*. An offence committed whilst the offender is already on bail must, by law, be treated as more serious by virtue of that fact.

Community sentences

The description 'community sentence', introduced in 1991, is an all-embracing term for the six types of community order discussed in *Chapter 3* of this handbook, ie:

- probation order (with or without added requirements)
- community service order
- combination order*
- attendance centre order (under 21 years of age only)
- curfew order*
- supervision order (under 18s only)

The items marked with an asterisk were novel at the time of the 1991 Act—and the curfew order has still to be brought into force nationally (trials in three areas commenced in July 1995).

Community orders are *sentences* in their own right. Even the probation order has been turned into a sentence (it was originally an order 'in lieu of sentence'). It was also common before 1991 to hear the more severe forms of community order, such as community service or enhanced varieties of probation order, described as 'alternatives to custody'. Strictly speaking, the only remaining alternative to custody to survive is a special form of supervision for offenders below 18 years of age. Magistrates should seek legal advice if asked to make such an order in the adult court.

The 'serious enough' test

A threshold was created whereby an offence must be 'serious enough' to merit a community sentence before any of the six community orders can be used—usually called the 'serious enough' test.

Restriction on liberty

The 1991 Act established a new impetus in favour of community based sentences, which were intended to restrict the liberty of the offender without the need to resort to a custodial sentence. It thus introduced the notion of 'restriction on liberty'. The restriction created by the order must be commensurate with the seriousness of the offence. Thus eg a probation order containing a requirement that the offender attend at a probation centre and take part in a programme intended to confront, say, alcohol or drug abuse, restricts liberty to the extent that whilst attending the centre the offender is not free to do other things—whilst the demands made by the programme itself (which may involve substantial changes in the offender's lifestyle) cannot be discounted.

Similarly, community service restricts liberty whilst the offender is doing unpaid work in the community.

Suitability
When passing a community sentence, the court must select the order (or orders) which is (or are) most suitable for the particular offender. Suitability thus has to be balanced with the restriction on liberty demanded by the seriousness of the offence.

Cumulative orders
The 1991 Act made it possible, in theory, for community orders to be made cumulatively—ie in addition to one another—provided that the seriousness of the offence justifies this. Great care must be exercised in relation to cumulative orders so that the overall sentence does not become *disproportionate*. There may also be technical or practical considerations and magistrates are urged to seek legal advice if considering such a course of action.

Probation and community service can only be combined in a combination order: see *Chapter 3*.

Custody
At the pinnacle of the sentencing framework is custody. For adult offenders, custody means:

- imprisonment in the case of an offender aged 21 or over
- detention in a young offender institution in the case of someone below 21 years of age.

The 1991 Act introduced three bases for custody. The first of these is, by far, the one most commonly relied upon in the magistrates' court:

- *The 'so serious' test*
In practice, custody is reserved primarily for situations where the offence is of such a level of seriousness that all other types of sentence are ruled out. The threshold test for custody requires the court to be of the opinion that the offence is so serious that *only* such a sentence can be justified—usually called the 'so serious' test.

- *The 'protection of the public' test*
In relation to custodial sentences for sexual or violent offences (see pages 32 and 54), the 1991 Act also introduced, by way of an

13

alternative to the so serious test above, the need to protect the public from serious harm from the offender in question. This may justify a custodial sentence irrespective of the seriousness of the offence. It may also justify a longer sentence (within the legal maximum). Where the protection of the public from serious harm *is* in the court's mind, there will often be sound reasons to consider committing to the Crown Court for sentence.

• *Custody on refusal of a community sentence*
Custody can sometimes be used even though neither the 'so serious' test nor the 'protection of the public' test is satisfied. This is where a community sentence is proposed by the court and the offender refuses to consent to it. But this only applies where consent is a legal pre-requisite. Similarly, custody can be used if an offender wilfully and persistently fails to comply with a community order once made.

The above points are expanded on in *Chapter 3*.

Suspended sentences
Once imprisonment has been decided upon—but not before—it can be suspended for one to two years (although *not* detention in a young offender institution). The rule, since the 1991 Act, is that there must be 'exceptional circumstances' to justify the suspension: *Chapter 3*.

Fines
The 1991 Act introduced a short-lived system of 'unit fines' under which courts related the seriousness of an offence to a number of units on a scale from one to 50, then multiplied that number by the offender's disposable weekly income. The Criminal Justice Act 1993 substituted a more flexible arrangement under which the size of a fine must reflect the seriousness of the offence. But the 1993 Act retained a power, introduced by the 1991 Act, to increase or decrease a fine according to the offender's financial circumstances. It also re-enacted in a new form a power to order the offender to provide details to the court of his or her finances (known as a 'financial circumstances order'). Courts must take such information into account when available: see generally *Chapter 3*.

A number of courts have continued to operate a (non-statutory) unit approach—as to which it is necessary to seek details locally.

Reasons for decisions
The 1991 Act (and subsequent legislation) has added to the situations in which magistrates are obliged to announce reasons for sentence-related

14

decisions and these are noted at appropriate points in the following chapters. Judicial decisions must always be based on sound reasoning, whether needing to be announced or not. This is why a structured approach to decision-making—as recommended in this handbook—is advisable. It ensures that all relevant matters are weighed and considered.

Early release
The 1991 Act introduced a new scheme of early release from prison (and from detention in a young offender institution)—a purpose being to create greater certainty about the proportion of time actually served under custodial sentences.

Magistrates acquired important responsibilities to deal with breach of licence and to return offenders to prison if they commit a fresh imprisonable offence whilst on release: for the precise situation see *Chapter 9*.

Enforcement
A feature of the 1991 Act was an improvement in the powers and procedures concerning the enforcement of sentences. Firm powers allow, eg for re-sentencing on breach of a community order. If the breach is deemed by the court to be wilful and persistent the court can treat this as tantamount to a refusal to consent to the order—which is a basis for a custody sentence: see above and *Chapter 3*. As already indicated, the early release provisions mentioned under the last heading allow magistrates to send or return offenders to custody.

'Section 95'
Sentencers have traditionally argued that a court should not be prevented from passing a given sentence merely because of its cost. Without attempting to introduce cost controls, section 95 Criminal Justice Act 1991 places a duty on the Home Secretary to inform sentencers of the '. . . financial implications of their decisions . . .'. Additionally, this same legal provision requires the Home Secretary to provide information to courts and others about discrimination on improper grounds. These items are dealt with briefly in *Appendix D*.

OTHER KEY DEVELOPMENTS

Since 1991, there have been a number of other key developments. The most significant of which are as follows:

Associated offences

Any number of associated offences can be taken into account when assessing seriousness. Offences are 'associated' offences if they are:

- offences of which the offender has been convicted in the same proceedings; or
- offences of which the offender has been convicted in other proceedings (by the same or another court) and which have now been referred for sentencing; or
- offences to be taken into consideration (TICs).

> References in this handbook to the seriousness of an offence should be understood to mean the offence and any associated offences which are relevant when assessing seriousness.

Earlier convictions and responses

Previous convictions and responses to earlier sentences can be taken into account when assessing the seriousness of an offence if relevant. However, great care is needed when considering how to apply the governing statutory provision, section 29 Criminal Justice Act 1991. This is the subject matter of *Chapter 6*.

Pre-sentence reports

The 1991 Act introduced the pre-sentence report or 'PSR'. So far as magistrates' courts are concerned, the underlying rule is that a PSR must be obtained before:

- deciding whether an offence is so serious that only a custodial sentence is justified and how long that sentence should be;
- deciding, in the case of a violent or sexual offence, whether a custodial sentence is necessary to protect the public from serious harm from the offender or whether a longer sentence should be passed than is indicated by the seriousness of the offence;
- making certain community orders (and, in particular, before considering whether they are suitable for an offender).

Although these obligations to obtain a PSR remain, courts can, as a result of the Criminal Justice and Public Order Act 1994, deem such a report to be 'unnecessary'. Pre-sentence reports are governed by a Home Office 'National Standard for Pre-sentence Reports' and are the subject matter of *Chapter 8*.

Credit for a guilty plea

It has long been the practice in the Crown Court to consider reducing sentences in appropriate cases where a timely guilty plea has been entered. The practice stems from the notion that a guilty plea indicates remorse or contrition, but it is also a device born out of expediency, ie a guilty plea saves time and public expense. The principle has operated at the magisterial level (see the notes to the Magistrates' Association *Sentencing Guidelines* in *Appendix B*)—albeit that the scope for reduction may be less than in the Crown Court, where more serious and lengthy cases may make it easier to assess what credit should be given. The case law indicates that, in appropriate cases, the reduction may be up to one-third of the sentence, depending on all the circumstances. Credit might not be appropriate at all in some cases, eg where the offender is caught 'red-handed' or has no real option but to plead guilty.

Under the Criminal Justice and Public Order Act 1994 all courts are required to consider the timing of a guilty plea and the circumstances in which it was entered. Where credit is given, the court must announce that fact.

SENTENCING IN CONTEXT

The next two chapters place the modern developments outlined in this chapter into context. *Chapter 2* deals with certain broad, general considerations which affect all sentence decisions, whilst *Chapter 3* looks in greater detail at the sentencing framework and the range of sentences available.

APPEALS

People who have been convicted and sentenced by a magistrates' court can appeal to the Crown Court against the conviction, sentence, or both or to the High Court on a point of law. Appeal to the Crown Court is the normal method of appeal, especially in sentencing matters. The offender must give written notice of appeal within 21 days of being sentenced, setting out the general grounds of appeal eg 'That in all the circumstances the sentence was too severe'.

The Crown Court can confirm the magistrates' decision or substitute its own sentence. This may be a less severe sentence or a heavier one—but limited to magistrates' maximum powers of punishment. An overview of the appeal process is contained in *Appendix F*.

Chapter 2

General Considerations

As outlined in *Chapter 1*, sentence decisions are made within a statutory sentencing framework—the central rule being that a sentence should be commensurate with the seriousness of the offence. The framework can be viewed as comprising the following:

- Four levels of sentence (see *Chapter 3*)

- The various statutory criteria whereby, for the greater part, the seriousness of the offence determines the level within which the sentence should be fixed—and the extent of that sentence

- The special considerations which attach to most sexual or violent offences, and which may lead to a custodial sentence—or a longer custodial sentence than would be justified simply by the seriousness of the offence—if this is necessary to protect the public from serious harm from the offender

- Provisions which require courts to consider relevant information (including, when appropriate, a pre-sentence report or PSR) and to adopt other procedures when passing sentence.

These items must be set against the wider background to sentencing law and practice as it has developed over the years—and within which it has always been assumed that there are certain 'general objects of sentencing'.

GENERAL OBJECTS OF SENTENCING

Historically, there have been six traditionally recognised objects of sentencing—which courts must try to achieve. These are:

- punishment
- reparation (including financial compensation to a victim)
- protection of the public
- deterrence

18

- reflecting proper public concern
- rehabilitation.

To these might be added a further aim: that of 'disposal', ie each offence requires its own sentence. On occasion, a minor form of sentence (a nominal fine or absolute discharge) may be appropriate simply to dispose of the matter. Also, the non-statutory practice of imposing 'no separate penalty' (NSP) has developed. This allows the court—usually in the case of multiple offences—to deal with minor matters without adding to the total sentence once the offender has been sentenced for the most serious offences at an appropriate level.

The extent to which traditional sentencing objects have survived the 'proportionate', 'commensurate' or the 'just deserts' approach, introduced by the 1991 Act (*Chapter 1*) can be summarised as follows:

Punishment
It is fundamental to the idea of 'just deserts' that sentences contain an appropriate, ie a commensurate, level of punishment.

Reparation
Making reparation, ie putting something back by way of acts intended to benefit the victim or the community is an underlying rationale of community sentences, particularly community service. The fact eg that an offender has made voluntary reparation may indicate remorse or contrition and thereby, depending on the circumstances, justify some reduction of sentence (see also *Credit for a guilty* plea in *Chapter 1*).

Compensation to victims of crime is one aspect of reparation and is a constant sentencing consideration. This is considered in *Chapter 4*.

Protection of the public
The object of protecting the public has emerged in a clearer, more defined manner in the special custody provisions affecting most sexual or violent offences: see *Chapter 3*. In relation to other types of offence, the need to protect the public may be a relevant consideration but cannot be used to justify a sentence which is longer than is commensurate with the seriousness of the offence.

Deterrence
In one of the first cases to come before the Court of Appeal following the 1991 Act, Lord Taylor, Lord Chief Justice, sought to clarify whether deterrent sentences were consistent with proportionality in sentencing, ie whether they had been superseded by the then new legislation. His conclusions can be summarised as follows:

- custodial sentences in particular are meant to punish *and* deter
- such a sentence—in having to be commensurate with the seriousness of the offence—had to be commensurate with the punishment and deterrence which the seriousness of the offence required (*R v Cunningham* (1993) 14 Cr App R(S) 386).

However, the Court of Appeal made it clear that increasing a sentence beyond the length which by those criteria is commensurate with seriousness to make an example of the defendant (sometimes called an 'exemplary sentence') offends the principle of proportionality.

Reflecting proper public concern
The Court of Appeal has retained, certainly so far as custodial sentences are concerned, the concept of a right thinking member of the public, in possession of all the facts, feeling that in certain cases justice could not be done without a custodial sentence being passed: *R v Cox (David Geoffrey)* (1993) 14 Cr App R(S) 619.

Rehabilitation
Rehabilitation has found a new place due to the emphasis on the suitability for the offender of community orders—and expressly as one of the statutory purposes of probation: *Chapter 3*. It is also an underlying rationale of the scheme under which prisoners are released on licence: *Chapter 9.*

THE TOTALITY PRINCIPLE

A further principle which affects all sentences is that, where there are a a number of offences, the sentences, in combination, should not be out of all proportion to the nature of the offending under consideration. What this means in practice is that when imposing several sentences at the same time—particularly if they concern the same events— magistrates should review the total effect and make any appropriate downwards adjustments.

STRUCTURED DECISION-MAKING

The Judicial Studies Board has promulgated the concept of making judicial decisions, and sentencing decisions in particular, by reference to a structure which can be represented by way of a chart or series of questions. Many structured decision making guides exist. An example appears in *Chapter 3*. Central to this process will be an assessment of the seriousness of the offence to ensure that the sentence relates primarily to the offence itself and is proportionate to it. This involves:

• deciding how serious the offence is in general terms, ie some offences (eg burglary) are inherently more serious than others (such as theft). This gives a starting point within the sentencing framework—or what the Magistrates' Association *Sentencing Guidelines* reproduced in *Appendix B* to this work call an 'entry point'.

• deciding what other, more individual, factors affect the decision—what are generally called 'aggravating' and 'mitigating' factors.

A main task is to weigh these latter factors to see whether, and to what extent, the offence is more or less serious than the general run of comparable cases. The *Sentencing Guidelines* begin by taking an 'entry point' for what could be considered to be an offence of average seriousness of its type. They then list particular ingredients which might be present and make a given offence more or less serious. The main purpose of guidelines—of which many local versions exist—is to encourage consistency of approach. The following is a general list, abstracted from the Magistrates' Association guidelines and the *National Mode of Trial Guidelines* (see *Appendix A*), of the kind of *offence* based factors which may fall to be taken into account:

—type of offence
—use or threat of violence
—use or carrying of weapon
—value of any property stolen or damaged
—extent of any injuries
—presence of racial motive
—vulnerability of victim
—offence against public servant acting in such capacity
—abuse of trust or power
—premeditation as opposed to spur of the moment
—prime mover as opposed to minor participant
—adult using children in commission of offence
—time and place of offence
—involvement of drink or drugs
—offence on bail

21

—immediate remorse or concern for victim
—offence of need as opposed to greed
—provocation

Additionally, certain *offender* based factors may affect the court's view of the seriousness of the offence eg: age, maturity, intelligence, health. However, these factors—along with such items as an early guilty plea or the offender's attitude to the offence (either of which may indicate remorse or contrition), efforts aimed at reparation to the victim, or co-operation with the police—are more typically viewed as 'personal mitigation': see under the main heading *Sentencing Information* below. The defendant's previous convictions and responses to earlier sentences can affect the seriousness of the current offence—but great care is needed in applying this rule: see *Chapter 6*.

Offences committed whilst on bail
Since 1993, a court is obliged by statute to treat an offence committed whilst the offender is on bail as more serious by virtue of that fact. The relevant provision reads:

> In considering the seriousness of any offence committed while the offender was on bail, the court shall treat the fact that it was committed in those circumstances as an aggravating factor.

However, despite the apparent strictness of the requirement, during the relevant Parliamentary debate, a spokesman indicated that:

> The Government do not intend that an offence committed on bail will always lead to a longer sentence. That would be absurd where the two offences are totally unconnected, or the second offence is a trivial one . . .

Prevalence of offences
The fact that an offence is prevalent may make it more serious. This can also be so within in a particular locality, but in either case it seems that a distinction must be drawn between the fact that an offence occurs frequently (which many offences do, so that the 'entry point' for sentencing should already reflect this) and what might be termed 'a real outburst' of a particular type of offence and one that is perhaps gaining momentum. Court of Appeal guidance has given examples of ways in which the prevalence of a particular offence can increase its seriousness: eg a spate of sexual attacks on women can increase fear among women generally in an area and limit their freedom of movement. The decision as to what effect prevalence has on the seriousness of offences is ultimately one for the court in the light of all the circumstances.

THE SENTENCING PROCESS OUTLINED

The categories of offence are set out in *Chapter 1*. With summary offences the court proceeds directly to the question of guilt or innocence and, in the event of a conviction, to sentence. Where the offence is indictable only, the court proceeds automatically with a view to sending the case to the Crown Court for trial.

With either way offences there is a preliminary stage known as 'mode of trial'.

Mode of trial

Magistrates must have regard to the following when deciding whether or not a case is more suitable for summary trial or trial before a judge and jury in the Crown Court:

- the nature of the case
- whether the circumstances make the offence one of a serious character
- whether the magistrates' sentencing powers are adequate
- any other circumstances which appear to make trial at either the Crown Court or in the magistrates' court more suitable.

These are all, to some extent, sentence-related items. On the basis of the prosecution version of the facts (which the court should, for the purposes of mode of trial, assume to be correct) and any representations by both the prosecutor and the defendant, the magistrates must, in effect, assess whether, in the event of conviction, their maximum powers—normally six months' imprisonment and/or a fine of £5,000 per offence; or 12 months in aggregate where consecutive sentences are passed for two or more either way offences—are likely to be adequate. Guidance on mode of trial is contained in the revised *National Mode of Trial Guidelines* (1995) reproduced in *Appendix A* to this work.

Where magistrates do assume jurisdiction, there is a residual power to commit to the Crown Court for sentence: see below.

The right to trial by jury

Even where the magistrates' court considers that an offence is more suitable for summary trial, the defendant still has an unfettered right, ultimately, to elect trial by jury in the Crown Court. In this event, the magistrates must proceed with a view to sending the case to the Crown Court for trial. Following a decision in favour of summary trial, the accused person is always asked whether or not he or she consents to trial in the magistrates' court.

Guilty plea and finding of guilt

The summary sentencing process only starts when one of two things occurs:

- the defendant enters a plea of guilty; or
- the magistrates find an allegation proved beyond reasonable doubt after hearing the evidence.

A guilty plea must be unequivocal, otherwise it has to be rejected and—if the plea remains the same after the defendant has had an opportunity to reconsider matters—a trial must be held.

The court must sentence on the basis of the facts of the case and any relevant information such as that contained in a pre-sentence report (PSR): *Chapter 8.*

Problems can occur in the following circumstances:

- *Guilty plea—facts contested*
The defendant pleads guilty but then suggests that the facts of the case—whilst still amounting to the offence charged—are substantially different to those alleged by the prosecutor, eg in an assault case punching and kicking may be alleged whereas the defendant strongly denies using his or her feet. Unless the prosecutor invites the court to proceed on the basis of the defendant's version, the court must usually hold a 'trial within a trial' to determine the true facts. This is known as a 'Newton hearing' (after *R v Newton* (1983) Cr App Rep 13, the ruling which established this procedure). The court must make a determination on the disputed facts, and should announce its finding, so that the rest of the sentencing process can proceed in the light of the facts found.

- *Conviction on a different basis*
Following a not guilty plea, the court finds the case proved but not on the precise basis alleged by the prosecutor eg the court may find that the defendant stole three items and not the ten alleged. In such a case the court will convict on the basis of three items and announce this. There are also cases, mainly in respect of road traffic offences, where a court hearing a not guilty plea is empowered, of its own volition, to convict of a different and lesser charge (eg dangerous driving reduced to driving without

due care and attention). Again, in such cases an announcement should be made so that the basis for sentencing is clear.

• *Self-defence*
There are cases of assault when the defence is one of self-defence and where it is for the prosecutor to disprove matters once properly raised by the defendant. If the case is nonetheless found proved it is essential for the court to announce, on convicting the defendant, whether it totally discounted any suggestion of self-defence or whether it accepted the need for some force but felt that the defendant had over-reacted.

Credit for a guilty plea
The court should always consider whether to reduce the sentence on account of a timely plea of guilty: *Chapter 1*. If it does give a reduction, it must announce the fact that it has done so—although there is no obligation to go beyond this bare statement.

SENTENCING INFORMATION

The prosecutor will present the facts fairly and objectively, but will not enter the sentencing arena save in limited ways eg by:

• providing details of any criminal record and 'antecedents'
• correcting misleading information
• where the court has a duty to make obligatory orders such as endorsement or disqualification, by reminding the court of this or countering suggestions by the defence that the court should refrain from making such orders (see eg the discussion of 'special reasons' in *Chapter 7*)
• contributing to discussion in court if there are doubts about whether or not the court has certain powers—but without seeking to influence the sentence decision
• making specific applications, eg for forfeiture of property, a weapon, or drugs (*Chapter 5*).

Once the basic facts of the offence are established, there begins a further information gathering process—which may involve questions from the bench. The aim is for the court to have before it as much relevant information as is appropriate to the case. The extent of the information will depend on the nature of the case (generally speaking, the more serious the offence and the more severe the likely outcome, the greater the need to explore additional items). The information might include:

Previous convictions

The prosecutor will provide a list of any previous convictions (courts should be alert to the fact that recent convictions may not appear on such lists). Defence advocates may have difficulty if they know that the list is incomplete. Whereas they are officers of the court, they also owe a duty to their client which would prevent their disclosing omissions without his or her express consent. Thus when defence solicitors are asked to confirm the list they may properly invite the court to put that question direct to the offender.

The list should be in chronological order and have marked on it any convictions which are 'spent' under the Rehabilitation of Offenders Act 1974. Statutory rehabilitation periods are automatically extended if another offence is committed during the initial rehabilitation period. However, courts can receive details of all previous convictions, spent or otherwise, and accord them such relevance as appears appropriate. The potential effect of previous convictions and responses to earlier sentences is considered in *Chapter 6.*

Antecedents

The list of previous convictions is sometimes called the defendant's 'antecedents'. Strictly speaking, antecedents are wider, including eg details about employment, family, regular financial commitments and so on—details being provided, if known, subject to local practice.

Cautions

The practice of cautioning (ie formally warning) offenders, rather than prosecuting them, is non-statutory and operates at the discretion of the chief constable of an area. Home Office circulars have sought to produce consistency. Normally, the decision to caution will have been made before a prosecution is launched, but the High Court has indicated that the Crown prosecutor must, when reviewing a case, consider whether a caution is preferable to continuing with the prosecution. In trying to set informal national standards for cautioning, the Home Office has advised that cautions should be cited to the court at the sentencing stage by the prosecution only where relevant to the offence under consideration and by way of a list separate from the previous convictions (see generally Home Office Circulars 59/1990; 18/1994). It is for courts to decide what relevance to attach to a caution. The offence will have been admitted, but without the protections afforded by a court of law. It will have been accepted as an alternative

26

to prosecution. But a caution will indicate that an offender has been warned about previous behaviour, possibly of a similar kind, and this may serve to cancel out mitigation which relies on ignorance of the effect of the behaviour in question.

Driving licences and DVLA printouts
It is essential for a court to see either the driving licence or a DVLA printout where a road traffic offence is endorsable or attracts disqualification from driving: see *Chapter 7*.

TICs
The non-statutory practice of defendants asking for outstanding offences—for which they have *not* been prosecuted—to be taken into consideration (known as 'TICs') is a means of encouraging offenders to 'make a clean breast' of matters and of disposing of possible further cases easily and quickly. The sentence should be seen to reflect any TICs and the court should make an appropriate announcement and keep a record of the relevant offences. The maximum sentence remains that for the offence *charged* (or the maximum aggregate sentence where there are two or more offences charged: *Chapter 1*).

An application should normally only be allowed where the substantive offences and those to be taken into consideration are either way offences (see *Chapter 1*) and of a similar nature. Endorsable offences should not be allowed as TICs, since the offender might escape 'totting-up' or a mandatory disqualification (*Chapter 5*). Usually, the prosecutor prepares a written list of the TICs for adoption by the defendant at the hearing. If he or she decides not to accept the list, or part of it, the court must disregard the list or part. The prosecutor then has to decide whether or not to bring charges instead.

Mitigation
The defendant or his or her legal representative will often put forward information in support of a request for a leniency—usually called 'mitigation'. A poor record reduces the scope for mitigation. Mitigation may relate:

- to the *offence* (in which case it should be considered along with other seriousness factors in arriving at the correct sentence level); or
- to the *offender*—often called 'personal mitigation' or 'offender mitigation', which can reduce a sentence below that which the seriousness of the offence alone would merit. Personal mitigation might include eg a character reference, a supportive

letter from an employer, evidence of excessive debts, ill-health or domestic difficulties.

The court must consider each case on its merits and decide what factors are relevant—as well as the extent to which these ought to be taken into account. It should be clear in the court's mind which kind of mitigation is under consideration, and its effect, if any, on the decision.

A legal representative mitigates 'on instructions' from his or her client and will not usually know whether the information supplied by the client is correct. He or she cannot (and should not be expected to) guarantee its validity—but must never knowingly mislead the court.

Written pleas of guilty—Section 12 Magistrates' Courts Act 1980

Where the prosecutor has adopted the written plea procedure in relation to a summary offence (usually known as 'MCA', 'section 12' or the 'guilty by post' procedure) all the information will be contained in the statutory documents: a prosecution 'statement of facts'; the defendant's written plea and any written mitigation; and occasionally a notice to cite previous convictions. The offender may address the court in person if he or she happens to attend. In either event, the mitigation can concern the offence or the offender's personal circumstances.

Financial circumstances

Where a financial penalty or compensation is in mind, the court can order the defendant to provide a statement of his or her 'financial circumstances'. The statement can be provided in writing or be given orally in court. There are criminal penalties for failure to provide the statement, or for giving false information: see *Chapter 3*.

Pre-sentence reports

The court may require a probation officer or social worker to complete a written pre-sentence report (PSR) to assist the court '... in determining the most suitable method' of dealing with the offender. This will require an adjournment, usually for three to four weeks. In certain instances, the court is obliged to obtain a PSR—unless it considers this to be unnecessary. PSRs are considered in *Chapter 8*.

Medical reports

The court can also order a medical or psychiatric report to inquire into the offender's physical or mental condition. Psychiatric reports are discussed in *Chapter 10*.

28

DEFERMENT OF SENTENCE

Deferment is designed to deal with the situation where—because of what a court has discovered about the offender—it considers that it is right to postpone the sentencing decision in order to 'have regard . . . to his conduct after conviction or to any change in his circumstances'. The defendant must consent to the deferment. The maximum period for which sentence can be deferred is six months. There is no power to remand an offender during this period and the court, in deferring sentence, cannot make ancillary orders except for an interim driving disqualification or a restitution order. It should be noted that:

- deferment may only be used *once* in respect of any offence. There are no restrictions as to the offence.
- the court must ensure that the offender understands exactly what is being proposed and to what he or she is being asked to consent.
- the interests of the victim must be considered. Postponing sentence may mean postponing compensation.

The offender must consent to the deferment, and the court must be satisfied, having regard to the nature of the offence and the character and circumstances of the offender, that it would be in the interest of justice to exercise the power. The Court of Appeal has given guidance as follows:

The consent of the defendant must be obtained . . . the court should make it clear . . . what the particular purposes are which the court has in mind and what conduct is expected of [the offender] during the deferment. The deferring court should make a careful note of the purposes for which the sentence is being deferred and what steps, if any, it expects the accused to take during the period of deferment.

Some specific object should thus be in mind. Deferment should *not* be used to avoid making a decision about sentence. Again, the Court of Appeal has stated that:

The purpose of deferment is to enable the court to take into account the defendant's conduct after conviction or any change in circumstances and then only if it is in the interest of justice to exercise the power . . . the power is not to be used as an easy way out for a court which is unable to make up its mind.

Guidance indicates that deferment should not be used simply in order to secure that which could be the subject of a condition of a probation order, eg continuing with a course of medical treatment. Care

29

must also be taken not to give an offender the opportunity of 'buying' his or her way out of a prison sentence.

Reasons
Reasons should be given to the offender about the purposes of the deferment—so that he or she is fully aware of what is expected during the deferment period. The court should also indicate how it wishes to be informed whether the offender has met its expectations—ie usually by way of an updated PSR.

End of the deferment period
It is desirable (but not legally essential) that the magistrates who ordered the deferment should sit to impose sentence. The bench should consider the reasons for the deferment and the nature of any expectations placed on the offender, and determine whether the offender has substantially adhered to what was expected. If he or she has done so, then a custodial sentence ought not to be imposed. If not, the court should state in what regard.

Further offence committed during the period of deferment
If the offender commits another offence during deferment, the court which convicts him of that offence may deal with the deferred case even though the period has not expired. If the court which deferred sentence was the Crown Court, then the offender should be committed back to that court to be dealt with.

COMMITTAL FOR SENTENCE

A magistrates' court can commit an offender to the Crown Court to be sentenced in a variety of situations. The most common of these is where he or she is convicted of an either way offence and the court is of the opinion that the offence (or the combination of the offence and associated offences) was so serious that greater punishment should be inflicted for the offence than the magistrates can impose—but in the case of a sexual or violent offence (see page 54) there is an alternative basis for committal, ie that a sentence of imprisonment for a term longer than the magistrates have power to impose is necessary to protect the public from serious harm from the offender. Accordingly, if magistrates are dealing with *one* either way offence, they will need to be of opinion that the offence merits a custodial sentence of more than six months before committing for sentence. Similarly, if dealing with two or more offences, they would be contemplating custodial sentences totalling longer than 12 months. In practice, committal is usually likely to occur only where magistrates believe that the sentence which the Crown Court would pass is likely to be significantly higher than one that they themselves can pass.

Mode of trial is discussed in *Chapter 2*. Decisions whether summary trial or trial at the Crown Court is more appropriate mean that the magistrates' court should have considered the main seriousness factors prior to accepting jurisdiction. Good practice suggests that magistrates should normally only use their power to commit for sentence to the Crown Court where some new material has come to light since the original mode of trial decision—such as the defendant's circumstances and any previous convictions (only presented after the defendant is convicted). But care should be taken that these do in fact affect the seriousness of the offence: *Chapter 6*. Other new information may emerge from the evidence in the case or because the full facts create a different impression to the original outline given at the start of the case by the prosecutor. However, the High Court has confirmed that a magistrates' court may commit for sentence if, on reconsideration of the original decision, the seriousness of the offence warrants a sentence in excess of their own powers.

An offender who is committed for sentence may also be committed to be dealt with by the Crown Court for certain other offences even though the magistrates' sentencing powers for these extra offences would otherwise have been sufficient (seek legal advice).

Magistrates may also commit for sentence: someone who is an absconder and who should have appeared in that court; on breach of an order or sentence of the Crown Court eg a community service order; or where the offender committed the offence during a Crown Court suspended sentence of imprisonment. Other circumstances include where a prisoner subject to early release (*Chapter 9*) commits an imprisonable offence during the original period of a custodial sentence and is liable to be returned to prison to serve more than six months.

Whilst there is power to commit for sentence on bail, the High Court has indicated that committal in custody is usually appropriate (it is somewhat incongruous to conclude that a defendant deserves a longer sentence and then to release him or her on bail. The general right to bail in the Bail Act 1976 does not extend to a committal for sentence).

Once the offender has been committed, any ancillary orders should be left to the Crown Court—apart, possibly, from an interim driving disqualification pending sentence (see *Chapter 7*).

The Sentencing Framework

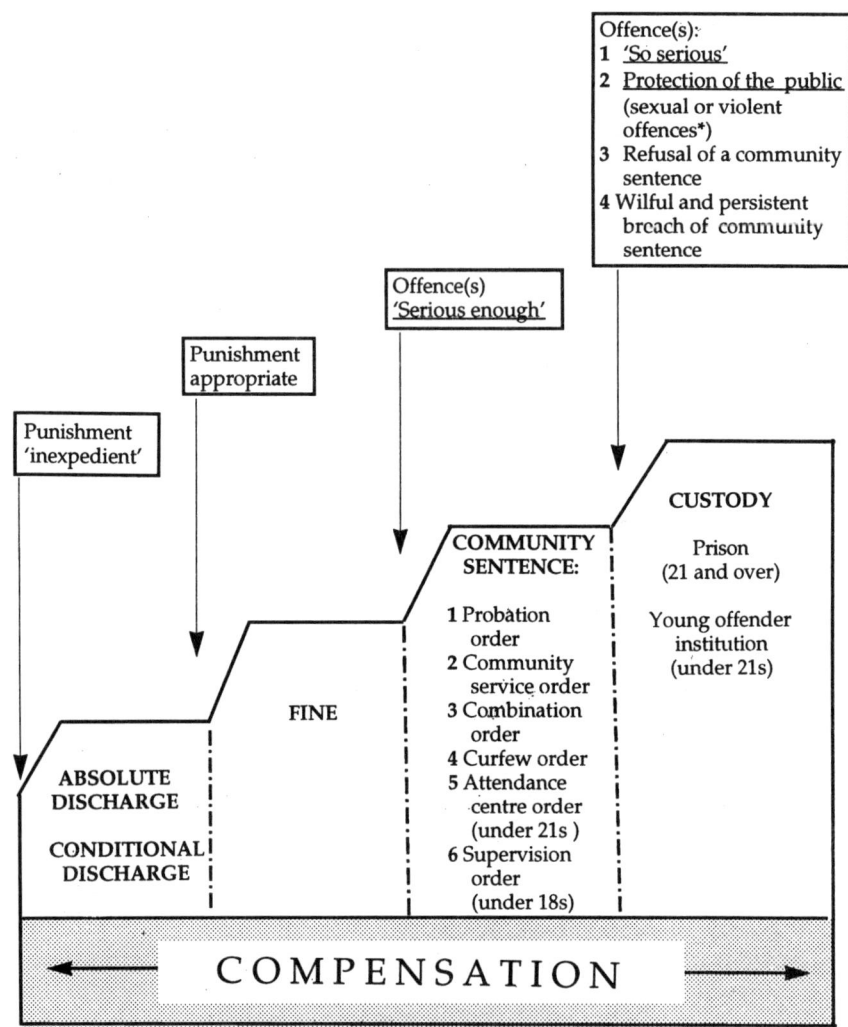

Offence(s):
1 'So serious'
2 Protection of the public (sexual or violent offences*)
3 Refusal of a community sentence
4 Wilful and persistent breach of community sentence

Offence(s) 'Serious enough'

Punishment appropriate

Punishment 'inexpedient'

CUSTODY

Prison (21 and over)

Young offender institution (under 21s)

COMMUNITY SENTENCE:

1 Probation order
2 Community service order
3 Combination order
4 Curfew order
5 Attendance centre order (under 21s)
6 Supervision order (under 18s)

FINE

ABSOLUTE DISCHARGE

CONDITIONAL DISCHARGE

COMPENSATION

Figure 1

*All references in this handbook to sexual or violent offences are to these offences as defined in the Criminal Justice Act 1991: see page 54.

Chapter 3

The Four Levels of Sentence

As indicated in *Chapter 2*, good practice indicates that sentencers should adopt a structured approach to decision-making. This chapter contains:

- a diagram of the *Sentencing Framework* (*Figure 1* on page 32)
- an explanation of the main elements of each sentencing option
- an example of a decision-making structure: *A Structured Guide to Sentencing* (*Figure 2* on pages 60 and 61).

THE SENTENCING FRAMEWORK

Figure 1 contains an outline of the sentencing framework which resulted from the Criminal Justice Act 1991 (as amended). It should be noted that each level of sentence is affected by statutory (or 'threshold') criteria:

- **DISCHARGES**: punishment is 'inexpedient'.
- **FINES**: by implication punishment *is* expedient (but more severe punishment is inappropriate). The size of a fine must reflect the seriousness of the offence.
- **COMMUNITY SENTENCES**: the offence is 'serious enough'. The degree of 'restriction of liberty' must be commensurate with the seriousness of the offence.
- **CUSTODY**: the offence is:
  —so serious that *only* such a sentence can be justified; or
  —if the offence is a sexual or violent offence (see page 54), 'only such a sentence would be adequate to protect the public from serious harm [from the offender]'; or
  —the offender has refused to consent to a community sentence proposed by the court and which requires that consent. Custody is also possible on breach of some community sentences where there has been 'wilful and persistent' failure to comply with such a sentence.

The length of a custodial sentence must be commensurate with the seriousness of the offence or, as appropriate, the need to protect the public from serious harm from a sexual or violent offender.

In most cases, the seriousness of the offence determines which of the four levels of sentence should be considered and the extent of any penalty. Any number of associated offences can be taken into account when assessing seriousness: *Chapter 1.*

DISCHARGES

> **CRITERION**: '. . . having regard to the circumstances including the nature of the offence and the character of the offender . . . it is inexpedient to inflict punishment . . .'

> **RESTRICTION ON LIBERTY**: none implied or arising.

Absolute discharge
This marks the conviction but no other obligations follow. An absolute discharge may be appropriate when the offence is of a truly minor nature, purely technical, or when there are several offences and a comparatively trivial one requires a residual sentencing disposal (which might equally be achieved by imposing 'no separate penalty': below).

Conditional discharge
This makes the offender subject to a single condition, ie that no further offence is committed within a period of up to three years—as determined by the court. Conviction of *any* criminal offence during this 'operational period' renders the offender liable to be re-sentenced for the offence which originally gave rise to the discharge—in addition to any sentence for the new offence. The court must explain the effects of the conditional discharge to the offender. There is no monitoring of the offender's behaviour or supervision during the period of the discharge.

Some people argue that a conditional discharge can be used at any level of seriousness, even instead of imprisonment on occasion eg to give an offender a fresh start. This depends on how courts interpret the phrase 'punishment is inexpedient' and whether this approach can be reconciled with the fact that, in the example given, the custody threshold will have been reached (though it is clearly established that personal mitigation relating to the offender can justify a less severe sentence when the seriousness of the offence might have justified a more severe one). Magistrates should check what view is taken locally and seek legal advice if faced with these or similar arguments.

Breach of conditional discharge

A 'breach' occurs if a fresh criminal offence is committed during the operational period. When the court comes to re-sentence the offender for the original offence, the seriousness of that offence has to be considered anew. Apart from substituting a different disposal, the court has the option of taking no action and allowing the conditional discharge to run if it thinks this is the proper course.

Breach of a conditional discharge imposed by a magistrates' court can be dealt with anywhere in England and Wales (subject to the consent of the original court if in a different place). Magistrates cannot deal with a Crown Court conditional discharge (but must inform that court of the breach) unless imposed on appeal from a magistrates' court.

FINES

> **CRITERION**: this is not directly covered by any statute. By implication, fines should be used where a discharge is not appropriate, ie where punishment *is* expedient—but a more severe sentence would not be. The *size* of a fine must reflect the seriousness of the offence.

> **RESTRICTION ON LIBERTY**: fines do not affect the physical liberty of the offender, but a loss of spending power deprives the offender of the ability to direct money towards recreation and leisure, or to choose how he or she spends a sum of money equivalent to the amount of the fine.

In magistrates' courts the maximum fine is set by statute, in most instances by reference to one of five standard levels. Values are updated by Parliament from time to time (currently, September 1995):

Level 1	£200
Level 2	£500
Level 3	£1,000
Level 4	£2,500
Level 5	£5,000

Fines for individual either way offences tried summarily are usually restricted to a maximum cash figure of £5,000. If no maximum is

35

specified (which is rare) then Level 3 applies. There is no over-arching limit affecting multiple offences (as eg there is with imprisonment). The global ceiling is, in effect, determined by the offender's own financial circumstances: below. Maximum fines in the Crown Court are often not subject to any legal limit.

Fixing the amount of the fine
This involves the court in the following tasks:

- an inquiry into the 'financial circumstances' of the offender
- taking these into account (so far as they are known or appear)
- reflecting the seriousness of the offence
- taking all other circumstances into account.

Financial circumstances
Courts can increase or decrease the size of a fine according to an individual offender's financial circumstances. Where there are several fines (and/or compensation or costs) the court must bear in mind the total impact on the offender's finances and may need to make downwards adjustments and/or extend the time for payment.

The term 'financial circumstances' appears to be wide in scope. It probably covers not only direct income but also eg savings, investments, endowment policies and valuable possessions, as well as permitting a court to consider the position of, say, an offender with no apparent income but who is living a fairly lavish lifestyle, based possibly on a partner's support which thereby reduces the need for personal expenditure. This last point is yet to be tested on appeal in the higher courts. The former law was against eg family income being taken into account.

Financial penalties should usually be set at a level which envisages payment within a maximum of 12 months (but possibly up to two or even three years in appropriate cases, particularly where compensation is concerned).

Financial circumstances orders
After conviction, defendants can be made subject to a 'financial circumstances order' (or *before* conviction if they have written pleading guilty under the written plea of guilty procedure: *Chapter 2*). The defendant is then required to provide such a statement of his or her financial circumstances as the court may require. This may be by way of written details or in answer to inquiries in court. Failure to comply is an offence punishable by a Level 3 fine (£1,000). False or incomplete

disclosure is a separate offence carrying three months imprisonment and/or a Level 4 fine (£2,500).

Combining fines with other sentences

Fines are capable of being imposed in addition to custody for a single offence. The general view appears to be either that a fine and a community sentence cannot be imposed for a single offence, or that this would be inappropriate. The possibility of a fine and a discharge for a single offence can hardly arise given the criterion for discharges (ie 'punishment is inexpedient', above). Ancillary orders can always be added to a fine: *Chapters 5* and *7*. A compensation order can be made on its own or combined with any other sentence.

If both a fine and compensation are considered appropriate and the offender cannot realistically be ordered to pay both in full because of his or her financial circumstances then the compensation order must always be preferred at the expense of the fine (and by implication any prosecution costs): see further *Chapter 4*.

Excise penalties

Certain convictions result in the imposition of an excise penalty rather than a fine. The most common example is the offence of using or keeping an untaxed motor vehicle, although there are many Customs and Excise offences leading to similar penalties. In these cases:

- the full amount of the penalty is payable unless mitigated by the court
- any excise penalties collected by the court will be paid over direct to the Commissioners of Customs and Excise unless the Commissioners direct otherwise (as they have done eg in respect of untaxed motor vehicles where penalties are paid over to the Lord Chancellor along with ordinary fines)
- excise penalties cannot be remitted in enforcement proceedings on account of a 'subsequent change in circumstances': see below.

Otherwise, generally speaking, such penalties are collected and enforced in the same way as fines.

Payment and collection of fines

Fines, compensation and costs are due and payable forthwith unless the court orders otherwise—and offenders cannot automatically expect 'easy terms'. Where appropriate, payment can be allowed by a fixed date or by instalments. Payment can be made in various ways including:

- cash (within the normal limits of legal tender, ie large amounts of small currency need not be accepted)
- postal order
- cheque (with or without a guarantee card. The court can refuse to accept a cheque if it has doubts as to whether it will be honoured)
- bank giro credit (standing order or *ad hoc* payments) if the court operates such a system
- credit card (if the court is experimenting with this method).

Payments are applied in the following order:

- compensation
- costs
- fine.

If the offender is already subject to a suspended committal order for non-payment of an earlier account (see below), that account will, in practice, be credited first unless the offender requests otherwise.

Remission and alteration of fines
A later court has power to remit a fine, in whole or in part, in the light of any subsequent change in circumstances. This will often be in enforcement proceedings. A separate power allows a later court to remit all or part of a fine where it was originally fixed in the offender's absence or without an adequate statement of financial circumstances if information before the later court suggests that, had the original court had that information, it would have fixed a lower fine or no fine at all. A compensation order cannot be remitted in the way that a fine can, but it can be discharged or reduced by a later court in limited circumstances: see page 65 and, if necessary, seek legal advice.

Immediate enforcement
The following measures are applicable to all types of financial order:

Power to search
On imposing the fine (or eg in enforcement proceedings) magistrates can order the offender to be searched—usually by a police officer or gaoler—and that any monies found belonging to the offender be applied to meeting sums due. Regard must be had to domestic needs.

Immediate custody

There are three circumstances in which magistrates can order custody in default (immediate or suspended as appropriate) at the time of imposing a fine:

- where the offence is imprisonable and the offender appears to have the means to pay forthwith (which might include withdrawing money from a savings account)
- where it appears that the offender is unlikely to remain long enough at a place of abode in the UK to enforce the fine by other means (eg a person of no fixed abode or who is about to go abroad)
- the offender is on the same occasion *sentenced* to immediate custody or is already serving such a *sentence* (ie not as a result of *committal* for some other default).

General enforcement powers

In all other circumstances the full enforcement process applies and a subsequent enquiry must be held into the default. It is often said that good enforcement begins at the point of imposition. If the size of a fine is assessed carefully and an appropriate order for payment made then, if there is default, there is also a sound baseline. On imposing financial penalties courts can set a review hearing date when enforcement will be considered if payment has not been made. Alternatively, computerised accounts programmes can respond immediately by way of a:

- reminder
- summons
- warrant backed for bail
- warrant without bail
- distress warrant.

Once the enforcement process is in being (and subject in most cases to the defaulter being before the court) there are various options:

- to set further terms for payment
- search (as described above)
- an attachment of earnings order (ie to an employer)
- a request to deduct the fine from income support
- a distress warrant to seize the offender's goods (either immediately or suspended on terms)
- an attendance centre order for defaulters under 21 years of age

- a money payment supervision order (usually operated by the probation service or a court's own 'civilian enforcement officer')
- detention in the court precincts or at a police station until 8 pm
- overnight detention in a police station
- imprisonment, or detention if the offender is below 21 years of age, within a scale which relates maximum periods to amounts outstanding. Either type of order can be suspended on terms
- application to the High Court or county court for civil remedies
- remission (above).

This handbook does not deal further with these powers. Advice should be taken, especially where custody is in prospect.

COMMUNITY SENTENCES

> **THRESHOLD CRITERION:** '. . . the offence, or the combination of the offence and one or more offences associated with it, [is] serious enough to warrant such a sentence.' This criterion applies to *all* six community orders below, ie the community sentence threshold must be reached *before* a particular order or orders can be chosen.

> **RESTRICTION ON LIBERTY:** all community sentences place demands on the offender's time, energies or activities. The extent of the restriction must be ' . . . commensurate with the seriousness of the offence, or the combination of the offence and one or more offences associated with it.'

> **SUITABILITY:** There is an extra (and sometimes conflicting consideration) in that the community order or orders selected must be the most suitable for the offender: see below.

Associated offences
The meaning of associated offences is set out in *Chapter 1*.

The six community orders
A community sentence is ' . . . a sentence which consists of or includes one or more community orders . . '. This enables courts to tailor

40

individual decisions by selecting one or more orders from the menu of six community orders, even theoretically for a single offence: but see further under the heading *Combining community sentences, below*. The six community orders are:

- probation order (with or without added requirements)
- community service order
- combination order
- attendance centre order (under 21 years of age only)
- curfew order
- supervision order (under 18 years of age only).

Restriction on liberty and suitability

Once the court is satisfied that the offence or offences are 'serious enough' to warrant a community sentence, two main considerations arise:

- The community order (or orders) must be the 'most suitable for the offender'
- The restriction on liberty arising from the community order (or orders) must be commensurate with the seriousness of the offence or offences.

There is thus a dual responsibility for the sentencer: that of deciding on the appropriate degree of restriction on liberty (as determined by the seriousness of the offence or offences), whilst ensuring that the community order or orders is or are the most suitable for the offender. This balancing exercise is one which makes considerable demands on sentencer's skills, and requires close attention if fair, appropriate and consistent sentencing practices are to be maintained. The statutory provision which creates these considerations mentions suitability *before* restriction on liberty. This is the only clue as to how any conflict might be resolved, ie possibly in favour of suitability (except where a 'suitable' sentence would involve greater restriction of liberty than can be justified by the seriousness of the offence).

Core issues

Thus, sentencers need an understanding of certain core matters:

- the factors inherent in each type of offence which are likely to affect seriousness, whether as aggravating or mitigating factors

41

- any personal and other factors which may be relevant to seriousness (eg previous convictions: *Chapter 6*, or in some instances the offender's circumstances: see page 22)
- what value to place on each of these factors so as to ensure a fair and consistent approach—taking account of good sentencing practice and local guidelines
- what each type of community order seeks to achieve and what demands it makes on an offender
- the comparative restriction on liberty which each of the six community orders places on the offender's liberty—and how these restrictions correlate in terms of duration, intensity, frequency and effect on offenders.

Liaison with the probation service
There is a need for a dialogue between sentencers and probation officers who write PSRs and supervise community orders—and hopefully an understanding on key matters. Many local probation areas and courts have entered into liaison on two broad fronts:

- by providing courts with detailed information about the nature and level of contact with offenders subject to community orders and discussing practice requirements for the service under the Home Office 'National Standards for the Supervision of Offenders in the Community'
- by agreeing a structure for common understanding about the relationship between levels of seriousness and the restrictions on liberty which arise from the various community orders (sometimes called a 'sentencing grid' or 'matrix').

Factors relevant to assessing seriousness
A note of some general factors affecting the assessment of seriousness is contained in *Chapter 2* under the heading *Structured Decision-making*.

Some factors relevant to 'suitability'
Bearing in mind the offender based factors already outlined in relation to the seriousness of the offence in *Chapter 2*, the following may be particularly relevant to the *suitability* of an order or orders for an individual offender.

—the type of restriction on liberty and effort or input required
—family or work commitments
—health issues

42

—age of offender

—the offender's mobility or lack of mobility

—perceived cause of offending

—the offender's own needs to enable him or her to turn away from offending

—the offender's general ability and motivation to undertake and complete the order

—the offender's consent and his or her willingness to comply with the order (which may be a statutory requirement: see *Chapter 3*)

—any risk of re-offending

—the protection of the public

—the prevention of future offending by the offender

—any responses to previous sentences by the offender and especially to community orders.

Combining community orders

A community sentence may contain (subject to one limitation) one or more of the six community orders. The limitation is that probation and community service can only be combined by way of a combination order. The extent to which the facility to combine orders might be exercised seems not to have troubled courts who appear, on the whole, to have adhered to the previous practice whereby there could be only one distinct disposal for each offence. In constructing a community sentence containing multiple orders the court must consider the overall restriction of liberty and be careful not to arrive at a *disproportionate* sentence. Legal advice may be desirable.

Despite the apparent intention of Parliament at the time of the Criminal Justice Act 1991, general opinion appears to be against using both a fine and community sentence for a single offence—although this is a possibility in relation to separate offences.

A probation order cannot be imposed at the same time as a suspended sentence of imprisonment, even in respect of a separate offence. This provision of the Powers of Criminal Courts Act 1973 survived the Criminal Justice Act 1991.

Ancillary orders such as compensation, costs, endorsement and disqualification can always be added to a community sentence. Compensation must be considered in appropriate cases: see *Chapter 4.*

Pre-sentence reports

In considering the question of suitability, the court must take into account any information before it about the offender. The court must normally obtain and consider a pre-sentence report (PSR) before deciding on the suitability for the offender of:

- a probation order with added requirements
- a community service order
- a combination order
- a supervision order with special requirements (under 18s only).

Failure to comply with this requirement will not, of itself, render the sentence invalid and, indeed, the court can deem a PSR to be 'unnecessary'. Good practice, nevertheless suggests that a PSR should normally be called for in circumstances where any form of community order is being considered: see generally *Chapter 8*.

Consents and explanations

The offender is required to express his or her 'willingness to comply' with the requirements of the following orders:

- Probation
- Curfew.

Other provisions require the offender to 'consent' to the making of the order:

- Community service
- Supervision with added requirements.

The combination order provisions (below) contain no express requirement in this regard, but the separate elements of that order (probation and community service) require willingness to comply and consent respectively. It is essential to ensure that the appropriate responses are obtained from offenders. Neither 'willingness' nor 'consent' is required for attendance centre orders.

Where consent *is* needed, a refusal enables the court to consider custody (assuming the offence carries imprisonment). This is the case even if the particular offence was not deemed serious enough for custody in the first place. If the situation is one of those where consent was required, custody can also be used on breach of the order: below. In the absence of authority to the contrary, the practice of courts appears to be to treat the terms 'willingness' and 'consent' as synonymous. The fact that refusal to consent to a community order can lead to a custodial sentence need not preclude the court from considering other forms of community or financial order to which the offender might consent, or for which consent is not required. But care must be taken to ensure that the offender is not seen to be dictating his or her own terms.

There is in respect of most community orders an obligation to explain to the offender the effect of the proposed order. This is good practice in any event—and a precursor to obtaining full and informed consent or an expression of willingness to comply.

PROBATION

The probation order is a sentence in its own right—and not, as was once the case, an order in lieu of sentence. A probation order can be made whether or not the maximum sentence for the offence includes imprisonment. The statutory purposes of probation are:

- to secure the offender's rehabilitation; or
- to protect the public from harm from the offender; or
- to prevent further offences by the offender.

Effect of a probation order
The offender is placed under the supervision of a probation officer for the area in which he or she resides or will reside. The offender must keep in touch with the supervising officer in accordance with instructions which the latter may give, and notify the officer of any change of address. These are sometimes called 'standard conditions'.

Duration
A probation order lasts for such period as the court decides—not less than six months nor more than three years.

Pre-sentence reports
Strictly, only probation orders containing additional requirements must by law be preceded by a PSR (unless the court deems a PSR unnecessary). Seemingly, most courts accept that it is usually undesirable to make even a basic probation order without full information.

Willingness to comply
Before any probation order is made the offender must express an informed willingness to comply with its terms.

Additional requirements

If felt desirable for any of the statutory purposes of probation (above) the court may insert one or more additional requirements ie:

• *a requirement as to residence.* This could be:

—residence in an approved probation hostel managed by the probation service or a voluntary organization.

—at a non approved hostel or other institution such as a dependency clinic which may tackle drug or alcohol addictions (some of which are private organizations).

—a requirement to reside where directed by the probation officer. This is likely to be in the offender's home area at a private address considered suitable by the probation officer and will restrict the offender from moving without first seeking approval from the probation officer.

• *a requirement to attend (i) a probation centre or (ii) other specified activities for up to 60 days*

—a probation centre is a resource approved by the Secretary of State offering an intensive programme which addresses offending behaviour and its various causes. Offenders are expected to attend for a full day and for as many days as is necessary (up to 60 days in all) to complete the programme. Probation centres are for those at the top end of the 'serious enough' scale.

—specified activities are approved locally by the probation committee. Offenders can be required to attend a specified activity—eg an alcohol education group—for up to 60 days or a range of activities according to their needs (eg an offending behaviour group, an anger management course, a substance misuse group). A 'session' lasting for, say, two hours counts as a day.

—there is one exception to the 60 day maximum rule and this applies to sex offenders. There is no upper limit on the number of days for which attendance can be required (subject to this not exceeding the length of the probation order), but the court which imposes the requirement must specify the number of days the offender is required to attend a sex offenders' group (or other facility) when making the order.

• *a requirement to receive psychiatric treatment.* This condition can only be used when the court has an assessment from a psychiatrist and treatment is actually available. Again, the requirement can be for the whole length of the probation order or for a part of this time as specified by the court.

• *a requirement to receive treatment for drug or alcohol dependency.* This refers to day or residential facilities—usually for the seriously addicted. There is no restriction on the length of the requirement. It can be for the complete duration of the probation order or for a specific part of it, as determined by the court.

Other requirements

Courts have a general discretion to construct other requirements to meet special needs within the overall purposes of a probation order. This discretion should not be used to circumvent any of the statutory requirements.

COMMUNITY SERVICE ORDERS

Under a community service order the offender is required to perform unpaid work in the community. A probation officer or someone employed by the probation service oversees the order. The offender must keep in touch with the relevant officer in accordance with instructions and notify him or her of any change of address. The offender must perform the hours as instructed, but instructions must, so far as practicable, not conflict with work, education or the offender's religious beliefs. The order has no inherent welfare content—and is mainly concerned with punishment and reparation.

Duration

The minimum number of hours is 40 and the maximum 240. The work must be performed within 12 months of the order being made, although the order remains in effect until the work is completed. It is possible to impose consecutive periods whether made on the same occasion or previously (legal advice is desirable).

Imprisonable offences

A community service order can only be made if the maximum sentence for the offence includes imprisonment. However, orders are no longer seen as 'alternatives to custody' but as sentences in their own right.

Pre-sentence reports and 'assessment'

A PSR is required before imposing a community service order unless the court deems such a report to be unnecessary. There is, in any event, with community service a separate requirement whereby the court must be satisfied that the offender is a suitable person to perform work under such an order and that work is available—usually called a 'community service assessment' (which, unlike the PSR itself, can be oral or written). Care must be taken as to what is said when calling for a pre-sentence report: see *Chapter 8*.

Consent
The offender's free and informed consent to a community service order is essential.

COMBINATION ORDERS

The combination order was created under the Criminal Justice Act 1991. It combines elements of the probation order and the community service order. This is the only way in which probation and community service can be imposed together for a single offence. There are no specific statutory purposes for combination orders, but the fact that the order incorporates elements of probation means that the purposes set out in relation to probation orders (above) are incorporated into the thinking behind that part of the order.

There is a single order even though the constituent parts will be supervised or monitored separately. The offender is subject to the same obligations for each part of the order as he or she would be if each had been made independently. Thus eg restrictions concerning the effect of the community service part of the order on work, education and religion equally apply.

Conditions can be added to the probation part of the order (see under *Probation order* above)—although attention must always be paid to the total restriction on liberty.

Duration
The order involves:

- a probation element of *at least* 12 months (as opposed to six months for 'straight probation') up to three years.
- a community service element of between 40 and 100 hours (as compared to a maximum of 240 hours for a free-standing community service order).

Restriction of liberty and suitability

The nature of the combination order means that care needs to be taken when assessing the extent of restriction on liberty and the suitability of what may be a particularly demanding order for the offender in question—especially if conditions are to be added to the probation part of the order. The outcome must not be *disproportionate* to the offence.

Imprisonable offences

The maximum sentence for the offence must include imprisonment.

Pre-sentence reports

A PSR is required before imposing a combination order unless the court deems such a report to be unnecessary. There is, in any event, a separate requirement whereby the court must be satisfied in respect of the community service element that the offender is a suitable person to perform work under that part of the order and also that work is available—usually on the basis of a community service assessment. This part of the assessment may be oral or written.

Consent and willingness to comply

Given the two separate elements, there is a need to elicit consent to the community service part of the order—and willingness to comply in relation to the probation part.

CURFEW ORDERS

The curfew order provisions are in force but of no practical effect until courts are notified that monitoring arrangements, electronic or otherwise, are available in individual areas. Trials began in three areas of England and Wales in July 1995.

Effect of a curfew order

The offender is required to remain, for periods specified in the order, at a particular place (usually, but not necessarily, his or her home) or places. Different places may be specified for different periods. The order is monitored by a person selected from a list of people specified for the purpose by the Home Secretary (and who may be drawn from the private sector).

If the court so orders, monitoring may include electronic 'tagging' of the offender.

There are restrictions comparable to those which apply to community service (above) concerning the effect on work, education and religion.

Duration
The order can be for between two and 12 hours a day which may be spread over one or more blocks. It can last for up to six months.

No need for an imprisonable offence
Curfew orders can be made in respect of *any* offence whether or not its maximum sentence includes imprisonment—although the 'serious enough' test for a community sentence must be satisfied and the court needs to consider, in particular, the extent of restriction of liberty.

Pre-sentence reports
There is no obligation to obtain a PSR. However, the court must obtain information about the place which it is proposed to specify in the order, and the effect that the order will have on people likely to be affected by the offender's presence at that place—pointing to the desirability of a PSR.

Willingness to comply
A curfew order cannot be made unless the offender expresses his or her willingness to comply with it.

ATTENDANCE CENTRE (UNDER 21s ONLY)

The purpose of an attendance centre order is that the offender be '. . . given, under supervision, appropriate occupation and instruction '. The order requires attendance at a specified centre and compliance with its rules. Centres are normally run by the police, sometimes with an input from other agencies. The regime is typically one of discipline, physical training, social awareness and social skills. A centre must be available to the court imposing the order and within reasonable travelling distance for the offender: below.

Duration and prerequisites
Attendance centre orders are available for offenders aged ten to 20 years inclusive, although there are separate junior and senior facilities. In the case of adult offenders (ie aged 18 to 20 inclusive) the order may be for between 12 and 36 hours. The court must fix the time of the first

attendance but the centre organizer determines the length of attendances and further dates. There is a maximum attendance of three hours on any one day.

Pre-sentence reports
A PSR is not a prerequisite but special attention should be paid to the following:

- The centre must be reasonably accessible to the offender having regard to means of access, age and other relevant circumstances (centres for females, or 'mixed centres' are less common than those for males).
- As far as practicable, attendance must not interfere with school or work hours.

Imprisonable offences
The maximum sentence for the offence must include imprisonment.

Consent
There is no requirement for the defendant to consent to the order.

BREACH OF COMMUNITY ORDERS

Each community order is a self-contained disposal. Re-offending during the currency of an order does not, in itself, amount to a breach. Different provisions apply to failures to comply with the different types of order:

Probation, community service, combination and curfew
Failure 'without reasonable excuse' to comply with a requirement of any of these orders can, on the matter being returned to court, result in one of the following outcomes:

- a fine of up to £1,000
- a community service order for up to 60 hours
- an attendance centre order (under 21s only)
- no action.

In each case the original community order continues to run. However, the court has the option to revoke the order and to re-sentence for the original offence. There is a requirement to give credit to the extent, if any, to which compliance occurred.

Where the original community order required consent and the failure to comply is found to be 'wilful and persistent', the court, on revoking and re-sentencing, may deal with the offender as if he or she had just refused consent to the order. This is a basis for a custodial sentence: see under *Custody*, below—even if the seriousness of the original offence did not in itself warrant custody (and assuming that the original offence carries imprisonment).

If the order was made by the Crown Court the breach, once established, must (except where the order was made on appeal against sentence from a magistrates' court) be referred back to the Crown Court if revocation and re-sentencing are to be considered.

Attendance centre orders

Failure to attend or comply with the rules of the centre may result in:

- a fine of up to £1,000
- revocation and re-sentencing for the original offence (or committal to the Crown Court if that court made the original order). There are provisions analogous to those for other community orders, above, whereby credit must be given to the extent that compliance has occurred, and allowing a custodial sentence to be imposed if the failure was 'wilful and persistent'.

SUPERVISION ORDERS

Orders placing offenders under the supervision of a local authority can be made in respect of young people below 18 years of age, usually by the youth court. Such orders can be made by the ordinary magistrates' court in limited circumstances: see *Appendix E* for details.

AMENDMENT AND REVOCATION OF ORDERS

There is provision for amending probation, community service, combination and curfew orders. These also cover revocation on application by the offender or supervisor if there is a subsequent change in circumstances. Revocation can be ordered on its own, or coupled with re-sentencing depending on the circumstances. In some instances a subsequent court, on sentencing an offender to an immediate custodial sentence, can revoke an earlier order but has no power to re-sentence for the original offence in such circumstances. Attendance centre orders have their own statutory code for amendment and revocation.

> **THRESHOLD CRITERIA**: there are three bases for using custody as follows:
> • the offence, or the combination of the offence and one or more offences associated with it, is so serious that *only* such a sentence can be justified (the 'so serious' test); or
> • the offence is a sexual or violent offence (both widely defined by the Criminal Justice Act 1991: but seek advice) and only such a sentence would be adequate to protect the public from serious harm from the offender (the 'protection of the public' test); or
> • following refusal to consent to a community sentence which requires such consent (or on breach of such a sentence for 'wilful and persistent' failure to comply with the community sentence which originally required consent).

> RESTRICTION ON LIBERTY: the restriction on liberty resulting from custody is obvious—in that the offender is deprived of his or her physical freedom. However, the offender will normally be released under the scheme described in *Chapter 9* after serving part of his or her sentence.

Associated offences
This has the meaning outlined in *Chapter 1*.

Meaning of custody
Offenders aged 21 years of age and over are sentenced to a period of imprisonment. For those aged 18 to 21 years the order is for detention in a young offender institution—when the *minimum* sentence is 21 days.

Imprisonable offences
The offence must be imprisonable. The statute which creates the offence will state whether the offence in question attracts imprisonment. Contrast a term of custody for failure to pay a fine (above) which can be ordered regardless of whether the offence itself carries imprisonment.

Procedural requirements
Before imposing a custodial sentence, the court must take into account:

- All information available to it regarding the circumstances of the *offence* or *offences*, including aggravating or mitigating factors.
- All information before it about the *offender* where custody or longer custody is being considered to protect the public from serious harm from an offender convicted of a violent or sexual offence.

'Sexual offence' and 'violent offence'—definitions

The 1991 Act lists those sexual offences to which the protection of the public ground for custody applies (the list covers most sexual offences—but not eg indecent exposure: in general, seek legal advice). Violent offences are widely defined so as to cover situations where an offence 'leads, or is intended or likely to lead' to death or physical injury (including arson). Protection from 'serious harm' means '. . . protecting the public from death or serious injury, whether physical or psychological'. Court legal advisors will normally anticipate situations where definition is likely to be a live issue.

Legal representation

There is a restriction on imposing custody (including a suspended sentence) where the offender is not legally represented after conviction and he or she is:

- under 21 years of age; or
- aged 21 or over and has never served a prison sentence (which does not include eg an unactivated suspended sentence, detention in a young offender institution or committal for contempt or for non-payment of fines).

The court should explain the effect of these provisions to an unrepresented defendant—with a warning to use the opportunity which the court is obliged to give by way of adjournment to acquire representation (if need be by applying for legal aid). Failure to obtain representation, to apply for legal aid, or refusal of legal aid on grounds of means will allow a subsequent court, if it considers it appropriate, to impose custody without the defendant being represented. An offender can waive these rights by declaring an unwillingness to consult a solicitor or to apply for legal aid—although it may be sensible to encourage the offender to consult the duty solicitor or probation officer before proceeding.

Pre-sentence reports
The court must obtain a PSR before deciding that either of the first two criteria for custody above (ie the 'so serious' test or the 'protection of the public' test) are made out—unless it deems a PSR to be unnecessary. The report is similarly needed in order to assess the appropriate length of the custodial sentence.

There is no comparable legal requirement for a pre-sentence report before deciding on a custodial sentence for failure to consent to a community sentence, or for wilful and persistent failure to comply with such a sentences (see above)—although there will need to be evidence of the failure and other relevant circumstances.

Care must be taken as to what is said when calling for a pre-sentence report: see *Chapter 8.*

Length of custodial sentences
Custodial sentences take effect straight away (and, where there are two or more such sentences, concurrently to one another unless the court has specifically ordered that they take effect consecutively).

The seriousness of the offence or, as appropriate, the need to protect the public from serious harm from the perpetrator of a sexual or violent offence should determine the length of any custodial sentence within the maximum sentence available. The protection of the public criterion allows a sentence longer than would be justified by the seriousness of the offence in respect of a sexual or violent offence.

The orders which are possible in the magistrates' court are as follows:

- imprisonment may be imposed for any period from a minimum of five days to the maximum available on summary conviction (this is usually fixed by statute at from one month to six months per offence)
- periods can be ordered to take effect consecutively to:
—previous sentences (ie those imposed on an earlier occasion)
—other sentences passed on the same occasion subject to the following limits:
  (a) six months in aggregate; or
  (b) 12 months in aggregate where there are two or more either way offences (see *Chapter 1*)
—a suspended sentence which is being activated.

The same limits apply to detention in a young offender institution (ie so far as offenders in the adult age range of 18 to 20 years are concerned) but subject to a minimum sentence of 21 days. The minimum sentence is designed to ensure that young offenders are not sent to custody unless the offence warrants more than a nominal period.

Concurrent and consecutive sentences

As indicated, magistrates can order custodial sentences to be served concurrently to one another or consecutively (ie within magistrates' maximum powers: above). The decision is a judicial one, and in the latter case, it must be clearly stated that the sentences are consecutive. In practice, sentences are usually ordered to take effect concurrently unless there is a specific reason for them to be made consecutive. This will primarily depend on the court's assessment of the combined seriousness of the particular offences under consideration, or, as the case may be in sexual or violent cases, the extent to which there is a need to protect the public from serious harm from the offender.

Short local detention

Where imprisonment is an option, the offender may instead be detained within the precincts of the court or at a police station for any period up until 8 pm (typically until the court rises). The offender must not be deprived of the opportunity to return home that day. None of the standard criteria, restrictions or pre-requisites apply. The power can only be used where the offender is 21 years of age or over. (Defendants aged 18 upwards may however be placed in short local detention for fine default or contempt).

SUSPENDED SENTENCES

Imprisonment (but *not* detention in a young offender institution) may be suspended for between one and two years.

The court must first be satisfied that immediate imprisonment is appropriate, ie that the 'so serious' threshold has been reached. A suspended sentence should never be viewed as some lesser, or intermediate disposal.

There must be 'exceptional circumstances' to justify the suspension. Case law indicates that the following *cannot* be exceptional circumstances: previous good character, provocation, youth, early guilty plea, domestic difficulties, loss of career, long public service, effect on pension entitlements (as these factors should have been taken into account as personal mitigation before custody was settled on). The Court of Appeal has interpreted the term 'exceptional circumstances' quite narrowly—although an example might be where an offender is in an extremely poor state of health.

Duty to consider a fine in addition
If the sentence of imprisonment *is* suspended the court must consider imposing, in addition, compensation and/or a fine.

Suspended sentences and probation
A probation order cannot be made at the same time as a suspended sentence of imprisonment, even in relation to a separate offence.

Commission of a further imprisonable offence
The court should inform the offender that subsequent conviction of an imprisonable offence committed during the operational period of the suspended sentence will render him or her liable to serve the sentence in full. In the event of such a further conviction, the court can adopt one of the following courses:

- the original period can be implemented for its full length (and consecutively or concurrently to any imprisonment for a subsequent offence). This is compulsory unless the subsequent court considers that to implement the sentence would be unjust in the light of all the circumstances, including the facts of the subsequent offence; or
- the original sentence can be implemented but reduced in length; or
- the sentence can be further suspended for any period up to two years; or
- the court can take 'no action'—a formal response (so that courts should not do this in the belief that the original court can still exercise its residual power to take action on the breach. This is especially important in the case of a Crown Court suspended sentence given that magistrates cannot implement such sentences but can either formally take no action or commit to the Crown Court, on bail or in custody, for that court to consider the matter).

Suspended sentence supervision orders
The Crown Court has power to make a 'suspended sentence supervision order' when it suspends *more* than six months' imprisonment for a single offence. Magistrates can in theory commit to the Crown Court for sentence with this possibility in mind (although there is always the risk that the Crown Court may use immediate

custody). The supervising officer will be a probation officer but the form of supervision, whilst containing certain elements similar to those in a probation order, is not the same and failure to comply with the supervision element may result in a fine but not in revocation and re-sentencing, nor activation of the imprisonment which was suspended. Only a further conviction can result in the imprisonment being implemented (on the bases already outlined above). Suspended sentence supervision orders never proved attractive to sentencers and have largely fallen into disuse.

Custody and mentally disordered offenders

Where the offender is or appears to be mentally disordered the court is obliged—in addition to the standard procedures for custody set out above—to:

- obtain and consider a medical report from a registered medical practitioner approved for the purposes of the Mental Health Act 1983 unless it considers such a report to be 'unnecessary'
- in any event to consider all information before it relating to the offender's mental condition; and to
- consider what treatment may be available.

Chapter 10 provides further general guidance on mentally disordered offenders.

Reasons for decisions

Whenever magistrates pass a custodial sentence they are required to state in open court:

- that they are of opinion that either or both of the 'so serious' or 'protection of the public' grounds for custody apply; and
- why they are of that opinion.

They must also explain to the offender in ordinary language why they are passing a custodial sentence. The reasons are specified in the relevant warrant and entered in the court register. There is a duty to give extra reasons where the court passes a sentence for a sexual or violent offence which is longer than is commensurate with the seriousness of the offence. Again, this must also be explained in ordinary language.

Clearly, all such reasons and explanations must be valid in the sense that they are properly relevant and supportable in law.

Magistrates should thus, as a matter of good practice, check their intentions with the court legal advisor.

EXAMPLES OF APPEAL RULINGS

The Court of Appeal sets the tone of sentencing practice, principally via appeal rulings in relation to sentences of the Crown Court—the resulting guidance being applied, often by analogy, to the generally lower levels of offence dealt with by magistrates. The summaries below give an impression of how the Court of Appeal approached some early appeals in the aftermath of the Criminal Justice Act 1991:

- Although the 1991 Act did not define or quantify seriousness in comparative terms, an offence might be so serious that only a non-custodial sentence can be justified where, to borrow from pre-1991 case law, '. . . all right thinking members of the public, knowing all the facts, would feel that justice had not been done by the passing of any sentence other than a custodial one.': *R v Cox (David Geoffrey)* (1993) 14 Cr App R (S) 479

- A short period of imprisonment (possibly 14 days) was appropriate for a motorist who in even a minor way assaulted another motorist in a dispute over driving: *R v Fenton* (1992) 13 Cr App R (S) 85. In another case, a sentence of six weeks was approved for a fairly similar offence: *R v Atkins* (1992) 13 Cr App R (S) 140

- A short period of imprisonment (less than 28 days) was appropriate for a female ticket clerk on a ferry who went equipped to sell old tickets and thereby to deprive her employers of fares (only £4 was mentioned in the charges). This was a clear breach of trust by an employee who also did not receive credit for a guilty plea: *R v McCormick* (1995) 16 Cr App R (S) 134. In contrast, a custodial sentence was overturned and a community service order substituted when a 19-year-old shift manager in a pizza shop stole a total of £1,080 from his employers on three occasions, mitigating factors including his youth and immaturity being taken into account: *R v Small* (1993) 14 Cr App R (S) 404.

- Where a longer term of custody is justified to protect the public from serious harm from the offender, this consideration has to be balanced with the need to ensure that the sentence is not out of proportion to the nature of the offence: *R v Mansell* (1994) 15 Cr App R (S) 771

For other examples see *R v Cunningham* at pages 19 to 20 of this handbook and *R v Wendy Bond* at page 77. Court legal advisors (*Chapter 11*) keep abreast of judicial guidance on sentencing. They are responsible for drawing attention to key rulings, guideline judgments and, if appropiate in a given case, to rulings falling 'on either side of the line'—so as to assist magistrates in arriving at the correct sentence.

A Structured Guide to Sentencing

To be considered in conjunction with:

- the sentencing criteria in this chapter (and *Figure 1* on page 32)
- the Magistrates' Association Sentencing Guidelines: see *Appendix B*.

NB Consideration of COMPENSATION pervades the whole process.

Consider the need for a PSR at appropriate points: *Chapter 8*.

Stage 1

DECIDE ENTRY POINT for an average offence of the type in question ie:
Level 1 Discharge
Level 2 Fine
Level 3 Community sentence
Level 4 Custody

Stage 2

REVIEW in the light of aggravating and mitigationg factors affecting the particular offence
MAKE INITIAL ASSESSMENT as to sentence level

Stage 3

Do previous convictions or responses to earlier sentences affect this initial assessment?
Was an offence committed whilst on bail?
REVISE ASSESSMENT as to level if appropriate.

Stage 4

CONSIDER whether, in certain situations, any matters concerning the particular offender affect the sentence level: see page 22
REVISE ASSESSMENT as to level if appropriate
Arrive at FINAL decision as to which level applies.

Stage 5

CONSIDER sentence WITHIN the level selected.
Do any of the following serve to reduce sentence *within* the level:
Previous good character?
Other personal mitigation ('offender mitigation')?
Credit for a guilty plea?

Fines: Consider local 'guidelines' and defendant's individual financial circumstances and revise up or down as appropriate.
Community sentence: Consider 'restriction of liberty' and 'suitability'.
Custody: Consider length of sentence (noting the special rules for violent or sexual offences).

Whether or not considered at *Stage 3:*
Do previous convictions or responses to earlier sentences affect the above?
Is there an offence on bail?

Stage 6

MAKE SURE COMPENSATION HAS BEEN ADEQUATELY CONSIDERED

Stage 7

CONSIDER the TOTALITY PRINCIPLE
Is the final sentence still proportionate to the offence or offences?
If you have departed significantly from the entry point at *Stage I*, check the reasons for this.

Stage 8

Obtain any appropriate consent, agreement or indication of 'willingness.'

ANNOUNCE SENTENCE including any ancillary orders eg disqualification, endorsement, costs, forfeiture.
Give any statutory (or other appropriate) **REASONS/EXPLANATIONS**

Note: Always check with the court clerk/legal advisor before making an announcement in all but the most straightforward cases: *Chapter 11*

Figure 2

61

Chapter 4

Compensation for Victims

In 1995 the Court of Appeal confirmed that the impact of a crime on a victim may affect the seriousness of the offence (*Attorney-General's Reference No 2 of 1995—R v Summerfield*: unreported when going to press). Relevant information may be contained in the evidence, the prosecutor's outline, or any PSR (which should also deal with the offender's attitude towards the victim: see *Chapter 8*). The term 'victim impact statement' is sometimes used to describe such information.

Quite apart from the fact that relevant factors may affect sentence as such, payment of compensation by an offender to a victim is an overriding consideration in many cases. As indicated in *Chapter 2*, reparation—of which compensation is an aspect—is one of the general objects of sentencing. In practice, magistrates are required and encouraged to award compensation whenever possible. Two factors are important:

- sensitivity to the interests of victims; and
- the extent of the financial information about the offender.

Priority
Where both a fine and compensation *are* considered appropriate, but the offender's means are not adequate to pay both in full, courts are required to give preference to a compensation order. It would thus be wrong to reduce the amount of compensation because of the defendant's means and then to impose a fine as well.

Where compensation and a fine cannot be imposed and where no additional form of sentence is considered necessary, compensation may be imposed as a sentence in its own right. Whenever it *is* coupled with another sentence compensation is described as an 'ancillary order'.

Legal position
Where an offence causes loss, damage or personal injury, the court is obliged by law to consider whether the offender should pay compensation. Personal injury includes physical or mental injury. An award can be made for terror or distress caused by the offence.

The magistrates' court limit is £5000 per offence. But the court can order compensation for loss, damage or injury caused by offences which it has taken into consideration (TICs: *Chapter 2*), as well as those in

62

respect of which it has actually convicted the defendant. The total is limited to the maximum the court could order for offences of which the offender stands convicted. If the offender is found guilty of, say, two offences and asks for seven others to be considered, the maximum compensation that can be ordered is £10,000 (ie 2 x £5000).

Application
There is no need for an application to the court (although the prosecutor will often make one on behalf of the victim). The court always has power to make an award—provided that there is sufficient information to enable it to set a figure: see also the reference to 'victim impact statements' above and under *Contents of a PSR* in *Chapter 8*.

If magistrates wish to make an order but require better evidence of the loss, damage or injury, it is appropriate to ask the prosecutor to obtain this information (subject to the victim's own wishes).

Reasons
The court must give reasons if it decides *not* to make an order for compensation where there has been loss, damage or personal injury. The reasons must be announced in open court and be recorded in the court register.

Straightforward cases
Magistrates should order compensation in straightforward cases where the amount can readily be assessed. The power to award compensation in summary proceedings represents—in those cases where the offender's financial circumstances are sufficient to meet the award—a speedy means by which the victim can be reinstated. An award by magistrates avoids the prospect of a separate civil claim by the victim in the county court or High Court.

Road accidents
In most cases compensation arising from road traffic accidents will not be ordered through the magistrates' court. However, an order can be made in respect of injury, loss or damage (other than that suffered by dependants as a result of death) due to an accident arising out of the presence of a motor vehicle on a road if it is in respect of:

- damage resulting from an offence under the Theft Act 1968 such as the unlawful taking of a motor vehicle (ie compensation may relate to the taken vehicle but not damage caused by it); or
- injury, loss or damage where

—the offender is uninsured in relation to the vehicle; and
—compensation is not payable under the Motor Insurers Bureau Agreement. This means that, in respect of property damage, the court is restricted to the first £175 of loss not covered by the MIBA (September 1995). But this may include any reduction in preferential rates (ie loss of 'no claims bonus').

Fixing the amount

When a court is considering a compensation order, it must satisfy itself that actual loss, damage or injury has resulted from the offence. The court will look at the cost of replacement or repair of goods damaged. Where items are of sentimental value it may be possible to draw common-sense comparisons with other property losses and the likely effect on the victim.

A court can consider loss of earnings following time off work due to a physical attack. It can also look at more intangible matters, such as pain, suffering and any loss of facility. Guidance contained in Home Office Circular No 53/1993 has, for the greater part, been adopted within the Magistrates' Association *Sentencing Guidelines* (for the relevant detail see *Appendix B* to this handbook). The guidelines set out suggested awards for a variety of injuries.

Usually the prosecutor and the offender/defence will try to agree the value of any loss. Where there is a dispute, the court will normally hear evidence presented by the prosecutor who may decide to call the victim to prove the loss, damage or injury, or this may be proved by other evidence such as a receipt or a medical report. The offender may then make representations and/or call evidence. The matter need not be proved to the same standard as the offence in a criminal trial (ie beyond reasonable doubt)—but there must be some factual basis on which the court can arrive at a figure.

Financial circumstances of the offender

Once the court is satisfied that there has been injury, loss or damage of a given value, its next obligation is to consider the offender's financial circumstances. It must have regard to these in so far as they appear or are known to the court. The Court of Appeal has interpreted this to mean that a compensation order should enable the offender to complete payment within a reasonable time, normally within 12 months. This can be extended to up to three years where the circumstances justify it. In many instances, the court will have required the offender to complete a financial circumstances form in relation to fines (*Chapter 3*). It cannot be over-emphasised that effective use of compensation often stems from the identification of financial resources which would enable the offender to meet an award—and giving compensation priority as required by law: see above.

In reaching its decision, the court may consider any savings or capital which the offender has and can also consider his or her expected income (sometimes called 'potential income'). Where the offender can afford to repay only part of the value of the loss, then the court can and should order payment of that part.

Where there is a suggestion that an offender might be able to sell property to pay compensation (eg a car) it is important for a court to consider a proper valuation. The offender's valuation may be 'over-enthusiastic' or inaccurate—or there may be other considerations such as an uncompleted hire purchase or credit agreement.

Apart from minor differences, compensation is enforced in the same way as fines are (*Chapter 3*).

Compensation ancillary to a custodial sentence
If the offender is sentenced to a custodial sentence there are obvious difficulties. The court will need to consider whether the offender has or will have the means to pay the amount ordered. The Court of Appeal has indicated that it is wrong to make compensation orders which will be a burden on release from custody, as this may lead to further offences to raise the money to pay the order. It is also not generally appropriate to combine a compensation order with a substantial sentence of imprisonment (eg 12 months) unless immediate funds are available. If the sentence is short then there would seem to be nothing wrong in a court ordering compensation of an amount which would not be considered burdensome on release, for example a sentence of imprisonment of three months and an order of compensation of £200 to be paid by instalments.

Appeal and review
The victim's entitlement to receive any compensation ordered is suspended for 21 days to allow the defendant time to appeal, or until after any appeal is heard. However, enforcement of the order against the offender is *not* suspended, since the obligation to pay arises immediately. In circumstances where an appeal is successful, the court will have to return any monies already paid by the offender.

A court can also review a compensation order at some future date at the request of the offender, including: where a civil court has decided that the injury, loss or damage was less than the value placed on it by the magistrates' court; where the property has been recovered; or where the offender's means have deteriorated (seek legal advice if necessary).

The choices for the victim

In theory victims can sue the offender for damages in the county court or High Court. Civil proceedings can be slow and expensive and an unwelcome further burden for victims. An order by magistrates provides the victim with a convenient and speedy remedy which avoids expense and delay—and represents a tangible expression of concern.

Typical decisions

Many decisions are straightforward and full compensation is ordered. However, from time to time, magistrates have to decide whether to order any compensation at all; how much to order; how to balance competing claims of victims and whether an offender with means should pay more than a joint offender without, eg:

(a) Offender A is long-term unemployed, on state benefit. He damages two plate glass windows value £1,000 each. The court has to decide how much compensation he can afford to pay by instalments out of his state benefit.

(b) Offenders B, C and D are charged with damage to property to the amount of £1,500. Offender B does not appear. A warrant is issued for arrest. Offender C enters a plea of guilty, is unemployed, in receipt of state benefit, and married. Offender D is single, working and earns £200 per week net. The Court has to decide whether offender D should pay the majority of the compensation or whether it should be apportioned evenly.

(c) Offender E, an adult, is being sentenced on a charge of assault occasioning actual bodily harm: an unprovoked attack on another motorist. The victim received two black eyes. The magistrates decide that in view of the nature of the offence and the offender's record, the sentence should be four months' imprisonment. They now need to consider the question of compensation to the victim. On the present guidelines, should they order the offender to pay about £200 compensation as well?

(d) Offender F, who is unemployed and in receipt of state benefits, pleads guilty to two charges of deception. The two separate victims are (i) an elderly pensioner, and (ii) a High Street bank. The pensioner has lost £600. The bank has lost £2,000. The magistrates need to decide whether the whole amount of compensation should be in favour of the pensioner rather than the bank, in view of the offender's limited financial circumstances.

GENERAL TREATMENT OF VICTIMS OF CRIME

In 1990, the government published a *Victim's Charter*. This outlined the rights of victims and stated how victims should be treated by the various agencies. In consequence, there have been improvements in the support given to victims of crime and more sensitive treatment.

The criminal justice services have also begun to improve the extent to which victims are kept informed of the progress of a case and given the opportunity to provide information to decision-makers.

Victim Support

A National Association of Victim Support Schemes (NAVSS)—now simply 'Victim Support'—was formed in 1979. There are local support schemes throughout most of England and Wales. The aim is to provide a comprehensive service for victims of crime, to raise awareness of the effects of crime and to work for changes which will assist victims. Referrals total around one million a year. There are some 8,000 volunteers and 700 full-time staff. The government makes a grant to Victim Support, amounting to more than £9 million in 1994/95.

Victim support schemes have a co-ordinator and a team of trained volunteers. The police give details of victims to the local scheme, which then contacts them to offer help and advice. They counsel victims and provide practical help ranging from assistance on household security to making insurance claims and applying to the Criminal Injuries Compensation Scheme: below.

Criminal injuries compensation

The Criminal Injuries Compensation Scheme, established in 1964, provides financial compensation to victims of crimes of violence and to those injured in attempting to apprehend offenders or prevent crime. The minimum award is currently £1,000 (September 1995) and injuries meriting lower awards cannot be compensated by the scheme. At the time of writing the government is taking through Parliament a Criminal Injuries Compensation Bill, which will replace the present scheme with a new 'tariff-based' system.

The original version of the scheme assessed awards on the basis of common law damages. Under the new scheme, injuries will be classified into 25 bands ranging from £1,000 (eg for an undisplaced nasal fracture) to £250,000 (for paralysis of all four limbs). There are procedures for review, culminating in a hearing by an independent appeal panel, which has as its members lawyers, doctors and others with relevant experience.

Chapter 5

Other Orders of the Court

In addition to the four main levels of sentence outlined in *Chapter 3*, magistrates' courts possess a wide variety of powers to make other orders. This chapter deals with a range of powers which are not featured elsewhere in the handbook.

BINDING OVER

Magistrates have power to bind over an individual to be of good behaviour and to keep the peace. The power—which stems from the Justices of the Peace Act 1361—can be exercised 'on complaint' (ie on the application of a public or private prosecutor) or as an adjunct to the sentencing process as eg where someone is convicted of assaulting a neighbour. Bind overs are a form of preventive justice. In effect, the defendant promises to behave or risks forfeiting a sum of money to the Crown (called 'a recognizance'). The order is made for a period set by the court, often a year. Refusal to be bound over is punishable by imprisonment for up to two months and/or a Level 3 fine (£1,000). Following principles of natural justice, the defendant should always be told what is in mind and be allowed to address the court before any final decision is made.

COSTS

Magistrates have power to award costs, subject to each case being dealt with on its merits. The basic rule is that costs can—and should normally be—awarded in favour of the successful party, including the Crown Prosecution Service. Costs must always be a reimbursement; ie they must not be used as a guise for punishment. Private prosecutors may receive an order that their costs be paid out of central funds (ie public monies held by the justices' clerk), but not the Crown Prosecution Service or other public authority—since they are funded out of the public purse.

Costs against offenders
The court can order an offender to pay just and reasonable costs to the prosecutor. The amount must be stated in the order. An order should only

be made where the court is satisfied that the offender has the means to pay. The amount must be stated in the order. Costs cannot be ordered if the offender has been ordered to pay a sum not exceeding £5 (whether by way of fine or compensation)—unless the court, in the particular circumstances, considers it right to do so.

The principles governing time for payment of costs are similar to those affecting fines. It is wrong to order an offender to pay costs if he or she will be unable to pay within a reasonable time (usually, in practice, within 12 months).

Unnecessary or improper acts or omissions
Magistrates may order all or part of the costs to be paid by either party to the other (called an 'inter partes' order)—irrespective of the final outcome of the case—if those costs have been incurred as a result of an unnecessary or improper act or omission, eg where one party forgets to warn a witness and the case has to be adjourned.

Wasted costs
Magistrates can disallow legal aid costs or order a legal representative to bear costs which are wasted. This means costs incurred as a result of any improper, unreasonable or negligent act or omission on the part of the legal representative (magistrates should seek legal advice).

Defendant's costs order
Where a case is dismissed, discontinued or withdrawn the court will usually make a 'defendant's costs order' (sometimes called a 'DCO')—ie for payment of his or her costs from central funds (see above). Only exceptionally will a prosecutor be ordered to pay the defendant's costs instead, eg where the prosecutor was negligent in failing to deal with some aspect of the case which would have disclosed a sound defence at an early stage.

A defendant who is on legal aid will not receive a defendant's costs order in addition to the legal aid order, unless this is to recover expenses not covered by legal aid (eg travel to court).

A defendant's costs order is normally made following an acquittal unless there are positive reasons for not doing so, eg where the defendant's own conduct has attracted suspicion and misled the prosecution into thinking that there was a strong case, or the defendant was acquitted on a technicality. Where someone is acquitted on some charges but convicted on others, the court has a discretion whether to make a defendant's costs order, or it might order only part of the defendant's costs. In this instance the amount must be specified by the court.

Unless the order is for an agreed or a part amount, the amount will be determined by the justices' clerk (as 'taxing officer') after the defence has submitted a detailed account.

RESTITUTION

Where goods have been stolen and someone is convicted of an offence relating to the theft, the court may order restoration of the goods to the person entitled to them (or of goods bought with any proceeds). Restitution can also be ordered on conviction for dishonest handling, obtaining by deception or blackmail. Goods include all property except land. An order can also be made in respect of TICs: see *Chapter 2*. An order can be made of the court's own volition (there is no need for an application) and may require:

- anyone having possession or control of the goods to restore them to a person entitled to them; or
- any other goods directly or indirectly representing the original stolen goods to be delivered to the person so entitled; or
- any money found on the offender not exceeding the value of the goods to be paid to that person.

The court may order restitution *and* compensation eg if property is damaged—but restitution should only be ordered in clear cases. Magistrates should avoid trying to solve difficult questions of law.

DEPRIVATION AND FORFEITURE

When the offence consists of unlawful possession of property, the court may order the defendant to be deprived of that property. A deprivation order can also be made where property has been used to commit an offence or was intended to be so used, whether or not the defendant has been separately convicted of that other offence.

The court must be satisfied that the property has been lawfully seized from the offender, or was in his or her possession or control when apprehended, or when a summons was issued. An order can also be made in respect of TICs: *Chapter 2*.

'Property' does not include land. The court must have regard to its value and the likely financial and other effects of the order on the offender (together with any other order the court is contemplating). The effect of the order is to deprive the offender of the property—which passes into the possession of the police. This enables the true owner to make an application to the magistrates' court for an order for delivery up of that property. If there is no successful claim, the property will be sold and the proceeds disposed of at the direction of the court.

Where the offence results in a person suffering personal injury, loss or damage and the court has not been able to make a compensation order (*Chapter 4*) because of the defendant's lack of means, the proceeds of sale resulting from a deprivation order can be used as compensation.

If an offender is convicted of an offence under the Road Traffic Act 1988 which is punishable with imprisonment (such as driving whilst disqualified or an 'excess alcohol' offence), the vehicle used is, by law, to be regarded as having been used for the purpose of facilitating an offence. Thus, the offender may be deprived of the vehicle once the court has considered all relevant factors, including the value of the vehicle and the likely financial and other effects on the offender.

Many individual Acts of Parliament provide for forfeiture of specific items on conviction, eg the Misuse of Drugs Act 1971; Prevention of Crime Act 1953 (offensive weapons); Obscene Publications Act 1964 and Firearms Act 1968. In some cases the court can also order destruction or disposal of the item concerned.

A deprivation order is appropriate only in straightforward cases where there would be no difficulty in implementing the order.

EXCLUSION ORDERS

Magistrates' courts have power to make what are termed 'exclusion orders' in the following circumstances:

Licensed premises
This variety of exclusion order is designed for offenders who make a serious nuisance of themselves in public houses. Accordingly, such an order would not be appropriate eg for a one-off minor offence by a middle-aged first offender. The order is *additional* to the sentence for the offence (which could range from a discharge to custody). The effect of the order is to prohibit the offender from entering the licensed premises in which the offence was committed or other specified premises without the consent of the licensee or someone acting on his or her behalf, such as member of staff.

'Licensed premises' means premises where a full justices' on-licence is in force (ie excluded are off-licences and registered clubs). The court must be satisfied that in committing the offence on licensed premises, the offender resorted to violence or offered or threatened violence.

The order may be for not less than three months or more than two years. A copy is sent to the licensee of each specified premises—and as a matter of good practice to the local police. The licensee or someone acting on his or her behalf may then expel anyone who has entered or whom he or she suspects of entering the premises in breach of the order. A police constable must, at the request of the licensee or staff, assist in expelling anyone the constable suspects of such a breach.

Somebody who enters premises in breach of an exclusion order is liable, on summary conviction, to a fine not exceeding Level 3 (£1000) and/or imprisonment for one month. A court by which a person is convicted of a breach of the order must consider whether or not the exclusion order should continue in force—and may terminate or vary it by deleting specified premises. An exclusion order is not otherwise affected by conviction for a breach of the order.

Football exclusion orders

Where someone is convicted of an offence connected with football, the court may make an exclusion order prohibiting him or her from entering any premises for the purpose of attending any prescribed football match. 'Offence connected with football' means:

- an offence committed at the ground or while entering or attempting to enter the ground in the two hours before the match, or leaving the ground up to one hour after it, provided the match is prescribed by the Home Secretary; or
- an offence involving the threat of violence or violence to a person or property or disorderly conduct or racial hatred on the way to or from any Association Football match; or
- an offence committed on the journey in breach of the Sporting Events (Control of Alcohol) Act 1985.

The court must be satisfied that the order would help to prevent violence or disorder at or in connection with prescribed matches. It must be for not less than three months (plus the unexpired period of any pre-existing order, or, if there is more than one such order, the most recent). An offender who enters premises in breach of an order commits an offence punishable by a Level 3 fine (£1000) and/or imprisonment for one month. The offender may apply to terminate the order after it has been in force for one year.

An exclusion order can only be made in addition to a sentence for the offence of which the offender has been convicted. For these purposes absolute and conditional discharges (see *Chapter 3*) count as sentences. The court may, on the application of the prosecutor, order a constable to take a photograph of the defendant.

Under the Football Spectators Act 1989, courts dealing with an offender convicted of football related offences can make a 'restriction order' for a set period. This requires the offender to report to a police station at a time when a specified match is taking place *outside* England and Wales. The court must be satisfied that such an order will help to prevent violence or disorder at or in connection with designated matches.

DISQUALIFICATION

Disqualification from driving is dealt with in *Chapter 7*. Magistrates must consider other types of disqualification in a variety of circumstances, eg in relation to:

Companies
Magistrates can make an order against an offender convicted summarily of an either way offence in connection with the promotion, formation or liquidation of a company, or with the receivership or management of its property, or a variety of offences in connection with company legislation (eg failure to file a return) prohibiting the offender, without the leave of the court, from being the director of a company or operating in other capacities within a company for a period not exceeding five years.

Animals
Magistrates have powers of disqualification in connection with various statutes dealing with animals, such as cruelty to animals where there is power to deprive someone of the ownership of the animal in question and to disqualify him or her from having custody of any animal. Legislation affecting pet shops allows magistrates in certain circumstances to disqualify an offender from keeping such a shop. Similarly, in respect of animal boarding establishments there is a power which enables magistrates to disqualify an offender from keeping such an establishment. Where someone is convicted of an offence in connection with the Dangerous Wild Animals Act 1976, the court may cancel any relevant licence held under that Act and may, whether or not the offender is the holder of such a licence, disqualify him or her from keeping any dangerous wild animal. In all cases, the period of disqualification is such as the court thinks fit.

Other disqualification orders

Other statutes cover such diverse topics as fishing licences, restaurant licences and gaming club licences. Under the Food Safety Act 1990, a court may prohibit the proprietor of a food business from participating in the management of any food business or any food business of a class or description specified in the order. There is also a provision within the Medicines Act 1968 which allows courts to disqualify an offender from using premises for a pharmacy for up to two years.

Notice

As a general rule, the defendant must be given notice and an opportunity to make representations before any disqualification is imposed. Prosecutions for some of the above offences are relatively rare, and it is therefore essential that magistrates seek legal advice.

DEPORTATION

Additional to the sentence for an offence punishable by imprisonment, the court may recommend to the Home Secretary that an offender who is not a British citizen, or a Commonwealth citizen having a right of abode in the UK, should be deported from the UK. The Home Secretary then decides whether or not to deport the offender. In coming to that decision, account will be taken of such factors as the nature of the offence, the length of stay in this country, previous convictions (if any), age, personal history, domestic circumstances and the strength of connections with this country. Any compassionate considerations and representations will also be taken into account. The Home Secretary is unlikely to deport a first-time offender unless the offence (allowing for any TICs) was particularly serious. This is a specialist area and legal advice should be sought, including in relation to European Community nationals to whom extra considerations apply.

Chapter 6

Previous Convictions and Responses to Sentences

It is part of the regular practice of the magistrates' courts for prosecutors to submit lists of previous convictions once someone stands convicted of an offence: *Chapter 2*. The relevance of the information contained in such lists turns on the true meaning of section 29 Criminal Justice Act 1991. The original section 29 attracted sufficient judicial and public criticism for the government to announce its replacement within eight months of the 1991 Act coming into force. The new section 29 governs the place in the sentencing process of:

- previous convictions; and
- responses to previous sentences.

It seems clear, irrespective of any legal rules, that if an offender has previous convictions, particularly if they are for similar offences, then this reduces the extent to which he or she can put forward mitigation. The offender cannot claim to have a 'clean record'. Similarly, if eg earlier community sentences have not been complied with this says something about the suitability of such sentences now: *Chapter 3*. But section 29 goes further. It is instructive to consider the background.

The original section 29
As indicated in Chapter 1, an intention of the 1991 Act was that courts should pass sentences proportionate to—ie 'commensurate' with—the offence or offences of which the offender stands convicted. The original version of section 29(1) thus provided that:

> An offence shall not be regarded as more serious for the purposes of any provision of [the sentencing provisions of the 1991 Act] by reason of any previous convictions of the offender or any failure of his to respond to previous sentences.

Section 29(2) then stated that:

> Where any aggravating factors of an offence are disclosed by the circumstances of other offences committed by the offender, nothing . . .

shall prevent the court from taking those factors into account for the purpose of forming an opinion as to the seriousness of the offence.

Thus, whilst previous convictions or responses could not affect the seriousness of the present offence, the facts of other offences which actually shed light on the current offence so as to make it more serious could. It was these provisions that attracted widespread criticism.

Common law principles prior to section 29 CJA 1991

Unpopular as section 29 was, there were those who thought that it merely set out the principle that an offender should not be sentenced for offences for which he or she had already been punished. The approach adopted by courts until 1991 was that whilst previous convictions might restrict or eliminate the mitigation which might otherwise reduce a sentence (above), a criminal record could not justify a more severe sentence, one *disproportionate* to the seriousness of the present offence.

Confirmation of the validity of such views can be found in the comments of Lord Taylor, Lord Chief Justice, in an address to the Annual General Meeting of the National Association for the Care and Resettlement of Offenders (NACRO) in November 1993. Lord Taylor suggested that common law rules laid down by the Court of Appeal before 1991 should still be regarded as valid.

The present section 29

In introducing the present provision into Parliament, the then Home Secretary stated that the original version had:

> . . . unnecessarily fettered the hands of the courts and imposed a strait–jacket on their ability to sentence justly in individual cases.

The present section 29(1) states:

> . . . in considering the seriousness of the offence, the court may take into account any previous convictions of the offender or any failure of his to respond to previous sentences.

The change of emphasis is clear. But it is not entirely obvious exactly how the provision alters the court's approach. In the public statement already referred to, Lord Taylor went on to say:

> I believe that the philosophy of the Criminal Justice Act 1991 as it was originally envisaged still holds good. I believe though, that the amendments [ie the new Section 29] have improved it and have made it more realistic.

Certainly, a defendant with no previous convictions might claim that the offence was less serious because it stemmed eg from 'a foolish, spur of the moment decision by someone with an otherwise unblemished record', whereas such convictions would, to the extent that they were relevant to the situation, limit or eradicate the scope for mitigation. It is less clear to what extent previous convictions can increase (or 'aggravate') the seriousness of the present offence—but, following basic principle, it seems clear that they ought not to be used to justify a sentence wholly disproportionate to that offence.

The relevance of past incidents
The new section 29 does not mean that *all* previous matters are capable of affecting the seriousness of an offence, and magistrates should always consider the relevance of previous incidents when sentencing. They should also be conscious about how much emphasis they place on the offender's record when deciding upon seriousness. The Magistrates' Association *Sentencing Guidelines* (see *Appendix B* to this handbook) offer the following advice to members:

> It is recommended that courts should clearly identify which convictions or failures are relevant for this purpose and then consider what the effect of such convictions or failures is in relation to seriousness.

Thus even where previous convictions or failures to respond to previous sentences of the court do affect the seriousness of an offence the question must always be answered 'To what extent?'

Court of Appeal guidance
Commentators on section 29 have expressed concern that it is now easier for the courts to send minor offenders into custody. It seems true to say that prior to the original version of the 1991 Act (above) imprisonment was sometimes a response to persistent minor offending and could not be justified by the seriousness of the present offence (see *Sentencing Practice in the Crown Court*, Home Office Research Study No 103, 1988). One general message from the Court of Appeal is that there are some offences which do not pass the custody test for seriousness, notwithstanding that the offender may have a long list of previous convictions for similar offences, eg a woman, already on a suspended sentence for burglary, using a false instrument and obtaining property by deception, was sentenced to three months' imprisonment for theft of bacon valued at £3.50 from a shop. The Court of Appeal stated that notwithstanding the breach of the suspended prison sentence, and a background of previous offending, the offence did not justify

imprisonment: *R v Wendy Bond* (1994) 5 Cr App R (S) 430. This suggests that there is a 'seriousness ceiling' for some offences which cannot be exceeded simply because of previous convictions.

Previous responses

An aspect of section 29 on which there has, as yet, been no judicial guidance is the impact of the phrase 'respond to previous sentences'. At first sight, it is difficult to understand how failures to respond to earlier sentences *can* affect the seriousness of the present offence. One view is that the provision refers to any conduct following the imposition of the earlier penalty. Another is that it refers to breach of an existing sentence or a further offence committed during that sentence: see *Chapter 3*.

Summary

If an offender has previously been convicted of other offences, or has failed to respond to previous sentences, this could rarely be taken into account under the original section 29. The Criminal Justice Act 1993 introduced a new approach. Courts *are* now permitted to consider the offender's record when assessing the seriousness of the present offence or offences—but must adopt a careful approach in assessing the relevance of previous convictions or responses to seriousness. There are areas needing clarification by the Court of Appeal eg:

- Should a court take previous matters into account if they are similar in type and/or recent, but not if they are different in type and/or were committed a long time ago?
- To what extent *can* previous convictions affect the seriousness of a new offence, ie does the current offence set a 'seriousness ceiling' and/or is the correct rule that sentence should not become wholly disproportionate
- Does a failure to respond to previous sentences include sentences which were completed without a breach or merely sentences which were breached, or still current at the time of a later offence?
- What is the precise connection between previous responses and the seriousness of the present offence?

It should be noted that previous convictions may be relevant to the 'protection of the public' test for custody in relation to sexual or violent offences for entirely different reasons. Unlike the 'so serious' test, the 'protection of the public' test involves an assessment of future risk (ie of serious harm to the public). Relevant past offences may be an important indicator of the extent of that risk.

Chapter 7

Road Traffic Offences

In addition to any penalty, certain motoring offences attract endorsement of the offender's driving licence or disqualification.

Endorsement
For many traffic offences, the court *must*, by law, order that the defendant's driving licence is endorsed with:

• particulars of the offence, and

• the number of 'points' appropriate to that offence.

The only exception is where the court finds 'special reasons' for not endorsing (below). Endorsement means that the above particulars and the sentence will be recorded on the licence. If the offender does not hold a licence, the order operates as an order to endorse any licence which the offender obtains.

Penalty points
Every endorsable offence carries a number of penalty points, from a minimum of two to a maximum of eleven. Some of the more common offences and their points are as follows:

Careless or inconsiderate driving	3-9
In charge (offences relating to alcohol/drugs)	10
Failing to stop after an accident	5-10
Failing to report an accident	5-10
Driving whilst disqualified	6
Using (or causing or permitting the use of) a motor vehicle whilst uninsured	6-8
Driving other than in accordance with a licence	3-6
Exceeding a speed limit	3-6
Failure to provide a preliminary specimen for a breath test	4
Failing to comply with traffic lights or traffic directions	3
Construction and use offences	3
Contravention of pedestrian crossing regulations	3
Using a vehicle in a dangerous condition	3

Appendix C contains a list of all endorsable offences and their points.

'Variable points'

Where the offences carries a range of points, the court has a discretion concerning the number to be endorsed —which will depend on the court's view of the seriousness of the offence.

Where someone is convicted of two or more offences *committed* on the same occasion, the number of points to be endorsed is usually the highest number attracted by any one of the offences. Thus eg if an offender is convicted of driving whilst disqualified (six points) and contravening a pedestrian crossing regulations (three), then six points would be endorsed. Instead of following this general rule, courts may add the numbers together ie making nine points in the example given. However, the court is obliged to give reasons if it adopts this course. The reasons must be announced in open court and be recorded in the court register. The chief significance of the system of penalty points lies in the 'totting up' provisions described under the heading *Obligatory disqualification* below.

'Special reasons' for not endorsing

As already indicated, when someone is convicted of an endorsable offence, the court *must* order endorsement and the relevant number of points unless it decides—on the basis of evidence—that there are special reasons for not doing so. The court must state in open court any grounds for finding special reasons, and these must be entered in the court register. A special reason means:

> a mitigating or extenuating circumstance, not amounting to a defence in law, but directly connected with the offence and which the court ought properly to take into account.

Special reasons must relate to the *offence*, as opposed to the *offender*. So, if the offender puts forward the fact that he or she was hitherto of good character and had driven for many years without being convicted of any offence, this would not amount to a special reason in law—since it relates to the offender. The onus is on the offender to establish special reasons and he or she must prove them on a balance of probabilities. If the licence is not endorsed, no points are imposed.

Additionally and quite separately to special reasons, there is a procedure with construction and use offences (eg defective brakes, tyres, steering) whereby endorsement can be avoided if the offender establishes that he or she did not know and had no reasonable cause to suspect the defect.

Special reasons and appeals

Where the offender is aggrieved by a decision to order penalty points despite his or her assertion that special reasons exist, there is a right of appeal to the Crown Court or to the High Court on a point of law. The prosecutor also has a right of appeal to the High Court if it is contended that the magistrates' decision is wrong in law.

Penalty points and fixed penalties

Where an offender has accepted a fixed penalty (below), there is no court hearing. If the offence carries a range of points (such as speeding, ie 3-6) the number of points imposed is the lowest of the range.

Disqualification from driving

There are two types of disqualification, *discretionary* and *obligatory*.

Discretionary disqualification

The power to disqualify an offender at the court's discretion exists whenever an offence is endorsable. A court considering discretionary disqualification should, as a matter of natural justice, warn the parties what is in mind. A discretionary disqualification may not be imposed for the same offence if the offender is also liable to be disqualified under the penalty points provisions (see *'Totting up'* below), and will not usually arise where the offence is subject to an *Obligatory disqualification* (see next paragraph).

Obligatory disqualification

Obligatory (or 'mandatory') disqualification arises due to:

- the nature of the offence; or
- the cumulative effect of earlier disqualifications; or
- most frequently in practice under the totting up provisions.

Offences for which the offender must be disqualified

There are several offences for which an offender *must* be disqualified (usually for a minimum of a year):

- driving/attempting to drive whilst unfit through drink or drugs
- driving/attempting to drive with 'excess alcohol' in the blood or urine
- failing or refusing to provide a specimen for analysis
- dangerous driving
- aggravated vehicle taking.

In all cases, the court *must* order the defendant to be disqualified for 'such period not less than twelve months' as it thinks fit—unless the court for special reasons (ie relating to the offence) thinks fit to order the offender to be disqualified for a shorter period, or not to order a disqualification at all.

The principles affecting special reasons have already been set out in relation to endorsement above—including the requirement to state the grounds for finding any such reasons in open court.

Where an offender is convicted of a drink/driving offence committed within ten years of a previous conviction for such an offence, the minimum period of disqualification is not one year but three years—unless the court decides, for special reasons, to reduce this obligatory disqualification, or not to impose one at all.

Cumulative effect of earlier disqualifications

A magistrates' court *must* impose a minimum disqualification of two years on an offender on whom more than one disqualification for 56 days or more has been imposed within three years immediately preceding the commission of the offence, if the offence of which he or she has now been convicted involves obligatory disqualification.

This means that an offender who is convicted of any of the offences listed under the heading *Obligatory disqualification* above and who has, within three years immediately preceding the commission of that offence, been the subject of more than one disqualification for a period of 56 days or more, must be disqualified for at least two years.

'Totting up'

In the main, the penalty points system is aimed at the offender who persistently commits relatively minor offences, and who ought to be disqualified because of repeated disregard for the law. Where a driver accumulates 12 or more points within a three year span, he or she must generally be disqualified for a minimum period (usually called a 'totting up' or 'penalty points' disqualification). In totting-up the points to be taken into account are:

- those falling to be endorsed for the offence before the court; and
- any that were endorsed on a previous occasion for offences committed within three years of each other, unless already wiped clear by disqualification under the penalty points system (ie previous totting-up).

When a court disqualifies the offender under the totting-up provisions, no penalty points are endorsed for the current offence.

Length of totting-up disqualification
The minimum period of a totting-up disqualification is:

- *six months* if no previous disqualification falls to be taken into account; or
- *one year* if one previous disqualification falls to be taken into account; and
- *two years* if more than one previous disqualification falls to be taken into account.

A previous disqualification falls to be taken into account if it was imposed within three years of the latest offence which brought the offender's points total to 12. It need not have been for totting-up (it could have been for an offence involving obligatory disqualification such as drink driving). However, it must have been for 56 days or more and must not have been imposed for stealing a motor vehicle, taking without consent, or going equipped for theft.

'Mitigating circumstances'
Under the totting-up provisions, the offender must be disqualified for one of the minimum statutory periods set out above unless the court is satisfied that there are grounds for mitigating the normal consequences of conviction and sees fit to disqualify for a shorter period, or not to disqualify at all. The onus of establishing mitigating circumstances is on the offender on the balance of probabilities. No account may be taken of:

- triviality of offence
- hardship, other than 'exceptional hardship'
- circumstances previously taken into account within the three year period.

Mitigating circumstances must not be confused with special reasons (above). The former are far wider in scope—and, in the ordinary way, they will mainly refer to the *offender*. The exceptional hardship put forward will usually relate eg to loss of livelihood if disqualification is imposed. If this plea succeeds and the court reduces the minimum period, or decides not to disqualify, then the offender cannot put forward the same ground again until three years have elapsed. Since

83

mitigating circumstances must be announced in open court and are recorded in the court register, courts can make enquiries as to what grounds were found at an earlier hearing.

Under the penalty points scheme only one disqualification is imposed irrespective of the number of offences. In the event of an appeal against any one or more of the offences, the disqualification will be treated as having been imposed in relation to each endorsable offence. The Crown Court has power to alter sentences imposed by magistrates for several offences, even if the appeal only relates to one of them.

Theft, taking vehicles without consent and similar offences
The general rule is that there can be no discretionary disqualification unless the offence is endorsable. But courts may impose disqualification in respect of offences of taking a motor vehicle without consent, stealing a motor vehicle or going equipped for the theft of a vehicle—despite the fact that these offences are not in themselves endorsable.

The rule against consecutive disqualifications
Disqualifications cannot be imposed on the same or a subsequent occasion to run consecutively to each other.

Disqualification in absence after notice
An offender cannot be disqualified in his or her absence unless first given the opportunity of attending an adjourned hearing. As an alternative, the court may issue a warrant for the arrest of the defendant (seek legal advice).

Commencement of disqualification
Disqualification starts from the moment it is imposed (credit being given by the DVLA for any interim disqualification: see under next heading).

Interim disqualification
The court has power to impose an interim disqualification when:

- committing the defendant to the Crown Court for sentence
- remitting to another magistrates' court for sentence
- deferring sentence: see *Chapter 2*.
- adjourning after conviction.

Accordingly, when eg a magistrates' court adjourns after conviction for a pre-sentence report (see generally *Chapter 8*), or a DVLA print-out (ie a computer record of the licence), it may impose an interim disqualification. The DVLA will reduce by the period of the interim disqualification the length of any disqualification imposed by way of sentence at the end of the case. An interim disqualification will automatically last until the case is finalised but, in any event, will not last for more than six months and the court has no power to make a repeat order for the same offence.

'Rehabilitation schemes'—reduced disqualification

Where a defendant is convicted of driving or being in charge when under the influence of drink or drugs, or driving or being in charge with excess alcohol in the blood or urine, or failing to provide a specimen, and is disqualified for a period of not less than 12 months, the court has power to *reduce* the period of disqualification by 3 months, or where it is for a longer period than 12 months by a period of not more than one quarter of its length—provided that the defendant agrees to participate in a rehabilitation course. Such an order can only be made where:

- the court is satisfied that a place on a course is available
- the offender appears to be 17 years of age or older
- the effect of the order is explained to the offender and that he or she is required to pay the fees for the course before it begins, and
- the offender consents to the order being made.

If the offender completes the course successfully and pays the fees involved, a 'certificate of completion' will be forwarded to the court and the reduced disqualification will take effect. Rehabilitation courses are only available in certain areas of the country at the present time (September 1995).

Disqualification until a test passed

When a court convicts an offender of any road traffic offence—for which disqualification is obligatory or discretionary—it can order the defendant to be disqualified until he or she passes a driving test. As long as there is no other disqualification in force, the defendant is entitled to drive a car but must display 'L-plates' and be supervised. If he or she drives without L-plates or supervision, then a charge of driving whilst disqualified can be brought.

The Court of Appeal has repeatedly emphasised that this type of disqualification is not intended as a punishment—but is to protect the public against incompetent drivers. Accordingly, the prime reason for considering such an order is the interests of road safety. Orders will generally be in respect of offenders who, through age, infirmity or the circumstances of the offence, display incompetence. Any court disqualifying someone for a long period of time and having misgivings about the offender's ability when the period expires may wish to also consider imposing a disqualification until the offender passes a test.

When the court convicts an offender of dangerous driving, it is not only obliged to disqualify the offender for a minimum of one year—but it must also order disqualification until a test is passed (the 'extended driving test'). This test is longer and more rigorous than the standard 'L- test', and enables testing of the driver in a variety of road conditions.

When an offender is convicted of an offence involving obligatory disqualification, or is liable to totting-up, and the court, in its discretion, decides to order disqualification until the offender passes a test, then the test taken by the offender is the extended driving test.

Removal of disqualification
Anyone who has been disqualified can apply to the court for the removal of the disqualification and, if successful, disqualification may be lifted from a date specified in the order. The offender may apply:

- if the disqualification was for less than four years, after two years
- if the disqualification was for less than ten years but not less than four years, when half the period has elapsed
- in other cases, when five years have elapsed.

If the application is refused, the offender must wait at least three months before reapplying. The court should have regard to the character of the offender and his or her conduct subsequent to the offence, the nature of the offence and any other circumstances.

The provisions do not differentiate between discretionary and obligatory disqualification. Many applications relate to offenders disqualified for three years for a second drink/driving offence within ten years (above). The offender can make an application for the return of his or her licence after two years have expired. It is suggested that magistrates should need a lot of convincing before removing a disqualification which an earlier court was obliged by law to impose.

Disease or physical disability
There is a mandatory provision of the Road Traffic Offenders Act 1988 whereby—in any proceedings for an offence committed in respect of a

motor vehicle—it appears to the court that the defendant is suffering from any disability or prospective disability, such as is likely to cause his or her driving of a vehicle to be a source of danger to the public, to notify the Secretary of State. There must be sufficient material before the court, eg something said by way of mitigation suggesting that the defendant is suffering from a relevant disability or a prospective disability. However, actual conviction is not necessary. Accordingly, a court might use this provision eg in respect of a defendant acquitted of careless driving because of a 'dizzy spell', or in respect of someone who is suffering from mental disorder and who is made subject to a hospital order without being convicted (see *Chapter 10*). The Secretary of State has various powers including to revoke the licence.

A note on fixed penalties

The time, trouble and expense involved in court proceedings can be avoided for some motoring offences by the police offering the alleged offender a fixed penalty ticket. This offer can be accepted by the payment of the fixed sum—when that is the end of the matter. If the matter is not dealt with in this way, then the usual result is a prosecution and hearing in the normal way.

The fixed penalty system has been extended to include a range of motoring offences, from simple parking to some that carry endorsement such as speeding, pedestrian crossing offences and construction and use offences involving tyres, steering and brakes. Where there is a range of penalty points (see above) and the fixed penalty procedure is used, the lowest number of points in the range is endorsed on the driving licence. The offer of a fixed penalty is a matter entirely for the police. The procedure depends on whether the offence is endorsable or not.

Offence not endorsable

A police constable (in this context a traffic warden may perform the duties of a constable) hands a fixed penalty ticket to the driver. The defendant has to pay the fixed penalty within 21 days to the relevant clerk to the justices (or within such longer period as is allowed by the ticket). The amount will normally be £20, unless the offence is illegal parking in London, when it is either £30 or £40 depending on the circumstances (September 1995). If the driver is absent, the constable (or warden) attaches the ticket to the vehicle.

If payment is made within the time limit, that is the end of the matter. If not—and no court hearing is requested—the police may serve a 'notice to owner' upon the registered keeper of the vehicle. This provides a fresh opportunity for the fixed penalty to be paid. If it is not paid, various things can happen:

- the person served may request a hearing (proceedings then commence in the normal way); or
- the person served may satisfy the police by means of a statutory statement of ownership that he or she was not the owner of the vehicle at the material time. He or she will then escape liability altogether; or
- if not the driver when the offence occurred, he or she can furnish a statement of ownership together with a statutory statement of facts countersigned by the actual driver. This will enable the police to prosecute the identified driver, if they wish to do so.

Driver present—endorsable offence
The officer requires the driver to produce his or her driving licence. Assuming that the driver is not liable to a totting-up disqualification (above), the constable can offer the alleged offender the option of a fixed penalty and invite him or her to surrender the licence. If the driver does not have the licence with him or her, the constable may give a provisional fixed penalty notice. The driver then has seven days to produce the notice plus the missing driving licence at any police station. If he or she does this and it is confirmed that no totting up disqualification is due, the offender will be given a fixed penalty ticket from that police station.

Requesting a hearing
Whenever there is an offer of a fixed penalty, the defendant can, within the stated time limit, ask for a court hearing. Proceedings are then conducted in the normal way, with the defendant being invited to plead guilty or not guilty.

Non-payment of a fixed penalty
If the penalty is unpaid at the end of the period allowed by the ticket, the fixed penalty (£20 non-endorsable offences and £40 endorsable offences) plus 50 per cent of this amount will be registered for enforcement as a fine at the defaulter's home court.

Conditional offer of fixed penalty
A conditional offer scheme is available for all fixed penalty offences (including those which carry endorsement). This allows the police to issue a notice by post to an alleged offender. They first issue a notice to

the registered keeper of the vehicle requiring information as to the identity of the driver.

The conditional offer is issued to the person identified by the registered keeper as the driver on the occasion when the offence was detected. Should the keeper fail to give information as to the identity of the driver, he or she commits an offence which is itself endorsable. If the driver wishes to take up the offer, he or she will send his or her driving licence and payment to the fixed penalty clerk named in the notice. He or she will accept payment subject to the driver's licence not disclosing that a totting-up disqualification (above) is due.

This relatively new procedure is being phased in—initially only in relation to offences detected by automatic devices.

DVLA printouts

After conviction and before sentence for any road traffic offence carrying endorsement, the court should obtain either the defendant's driving licence or a printout of the defendant's driving record. Printouts are necessary in all cases where the defendant's licence cannot be obtained—or one has not been issued. They are obtained from the Driver and Vehicle Licensing Authority (DVLA), Swansea, and contain details of the offender and any endorsable offences that he or she has been convicted of plus a note of any driving disqualifications. The printout also shows the sentences and court details.

Some courts operate a 'magnetic tape interchange' whereby they simply put the information on to a magnetic tape via computer, then post the tape to the DVLA which transcribes it and sends back the relevant printouts. This means that the period of any adjournment can be kept short. In other instances, it normally takes about three to four weeks to obtain a printout. However, where a defendant appears before the court in custody, then rather than delay sentencing, a designated officer of the court can apply for an expedited printout by telephone. This will then be transmitted to the court by facsimile.

Chapter 8

Pre–sentence Reports

A central decision-making tool in relation to more serious offences is the pre-sentence report or 'PSR'. Prior to the Criminal Justice Act 1991, courts used reports prepared by the probation service or social services—and known as 'social enquiry reports'. The 1991 Act renamed these and introduced a more defined and structured approach. At the same time, the preparation and content of reports became subject to a Home Office 'National Standard for Pre-sentence Reports'.

BASIC PRINCIPLES

A pre–sentence report is a report *in writing* which:

(a) with a view to assisting the court in determining the most suitable method of dealing with an offender, is made or submitted by a probation officer or by a social worker of a local authority social services department; and
   (b) contains information as to such matters, presented in such manner, as may be prescribed by . . . rules made by the Secretary of State.

To date, no rules have been made—but the National Standard mentioned above has filled this void. PSRs in the magistrates' courts are usually prepared within a maximum of 15 working days.

The obligation to consider a PSR
The court *must* consider a PSR when contemplating a custodial sentence or most varieties of community sentence: see *Chapter 3*. However, this rule was relaxed in 1993 so that there is now a general discretion to dispense with a PSR if the court dealing with a given case deems one to be 'unnecessary.' Sentences are not invalidated by the failure of the court to obtain a PSR—although any court on an appeal against sentence must obtain a PSR if one was not obtained by the court below (subject to the same discretion to deem this unnecessary). For all practical purposes, the former strict legal requirements have thus been replaced by good sentencing practice—which dictates that a PSR is appropriate whenever a court is considering any of the more severe forms of sentence unless the report could have no real effect on the

court's decision. The situations in which this can be predicted with certainty in the magistrates' court are rare.

In cases where a PSR is obtained, it forms part of the relevant information which a court should consider before deciding on such important matters as the seriousness of the offence or offences, restriction of liberty and suitability for a particular community order. Among other things, PSRs contain information about what demands will be made on the offender by a given sentence. PSRs are also relevant in relation to the risk of the offender re-offending—both generally, but more particularly in relation to the protection of the public from serious harm from the offender where the court is dealing with a sexual or violent offence.

PREPARATION OF THE REPORT

Once a PSR is ordered and an adjournment allowed for it to be prepared (usually three or four weeks), the report writer will aim to produce a report which is impartial, balanced and factually accurate. The writer will bear in mind that the report is for the court alone, and that it does not represent the interests of any individual or organization. He or she will provide a professional assessment of the case—the nature and the cause of the offence or offences and a note of any action which can be taken to reduce re–offending.

The National Standard confirms that a PSR must always be provided if requested by a court; this despite the fact that an offender might refuse to assist in its preparation. The writer will aim to produce the most useful report possible, ensuring that the offender was offered at least two opportunities for an appointment. The writer will, in any event, take all reasonable steps to obtain available, relevant information about the offender and his or her circumstances.

In addition, he or she will normally check whether the offender is due to appear on other matters, so that sentencing matters can take place at the same time. There is currently (September 1995) a practical difficulty, in that information may not be readily available until the Phoenix Criminal Justice Record Service is operational.

CONTENTS OF THE PSR

To accord with the National Standard, a PSR should be clear, concise, free of jargon, coherent and accurate in grammar, syntax and spelling. It

91

will start by setting out basic information on a front sheet, following which information will appear under the following main headings :

- An introduction
- Offence analysis
- Relevant information about the offender
- An assessment of the risk to the public of re–offending
- A conclusion.

The introduction
This will include a summary of the sources drawn upon to prepare the report, identify steps taken to verify information and, if appropriate, draw attention to any other potentially useful sources to which it was not possible to have access. If the writer is doubtful about any information, this will be noted. The report should also state whether the offender is known to the writer, the probation service or social services, and the number of interviews undertaken in preparing the report.

Offence analysis
This will normally include:

- an analysis of the offence or offences, including an assessment of the offender's culpability and the degree of premeditation
- information about aggravating or mitigating features of the offence which might assist the court when assessing seriousness (the PSR will not actually use the terminology of aggravation or mitigation)
- an assessment of the context of the offence, including information about any relevant associated offences
- a note of the offender's motivation, with the aim of helping the court to understand why the offender committed the offence or offences
- an assessment of the consequences of the offence ie the actual damage, injury, harm, cost of the offending (including the impact on the victim: see next point and, generally, *Chapter 4*)
- an assessment of the offender's attitude to the victim, the offence, awareness of its consequences, any expressed remorse or guilt and any desire to make reparation and/or provide compensation
- an assessment of any special circumstances eg family crisis, alcohol, drugs, physical or mental health directly relevant to the offending. The report will draw attention to ways in which these might be relevant to 'seriousness'

- where there is a specific feature of the offence which seems to conform to a pattern of previous offending (eg targeting vulnerable victims) this should be included.

Seriousness of the offence

As part of the offence analysis, the report writer will form a view about how serious the offence is—so as to ensure that the restriction of liberty contained in any proposed community sentence is commensurate with the offence. The writer will be steered by any provisional indications of seriousness given by the court: below.

Information about the offender

This part of the report is critically relevant to assessing the suitability of particular community orders for the offender. It summarises the offender's personal and social circumstances and evaluates any patterns of offending identified in the light of the personal or social factors which have contributed to them. This part of the PSR covers offending history and deals with issues of relevance to section 29 Criminal Justice Act 1991 with regard to previous convictions or failures to respond to earlier sentences (see *Chapter 6*). The assessment should refer both to positive and negative results eg successful completion of earlier sentences or breach of an order or a further offence committed whilst subject to a previous community sentence. Partial successes on which future sentences might build are also highlighted.

Ultimately, the report will give a balanced picture of the offender, both good and bad, and should note any positive action taken by the offender since the offence was committed.

The desirability or otherwise of a medical or psychiatric report (see *Chapter 10*) is also covered. If appropriate, the report writer will invite the court at the earliest opportunity to consider ordering one. Whilst the National Standard does not make reference to the point, it is good practice for the probation officer to endeavour to liaise with the author of the medical report when preparing the PSR, otherwise there is a risk of the two reports being at odds with each other.

Risk to the public of re-offending

The report writer will consider the risk of re–offending and the risk of harm to the public, including the risk of serious harm in relation to any sexual or violent offences for which a more severe or longer sentence might be passed (*Chapter 3*). This risk element has two dimensions—the nature and seriousness of possible future offences, and the likelihood of their occurring. This is a relatively novel area of work for probation officers and it remains to be seen whether defence advocates may sometimes object to what may be seen as 'speculative' views expressed in a report, or question the evidence upon which predictions are based.

The conclusion
The conclusion in the PSR should flow logically and directly from the rest of the report. The National Standard indicates that unless the offence is 'so serious' that a custodial sentence is inevitable, or not 'serious enough' for a community sentence, this part of the report should propose a community order which contains a degree of restriction on liberty matching the seriousness of the offence. Where the conclusion indicates that a programme can be arranged, the report should contain a proposal and invite the court to consider the merits. If not, the report should make it clear that a programme cannot be proposed, and why. Where the proposal envisages a probation order, any non-standard requirements (often called 'additional requirements') should be set out in the terms proposed.

Where the PSR envisages a probation order or combination order, it should contain an outline of the proposed supervision plan. When community orders are proposed, there should eg be a description of the purposes and desired outcomes, the methods to be used, a timetable with targets for achieving objectives, a note of the proposed frequency of contact with the offender, of when community service work will take place, and the likely effect on other members of the family. The description of any proposed programme should indicate the degree of restriction of liberty involved, how the disposal will help tackle the behaviour which led to the offence and the steps to be taken if the offender does not comply. Where a community sentence requiring consent is proposed, the report should state whether or not the offender appears to be willing to comply.

Unless the court has specifically asked for the report to cover a number of options, any proposal will be for a single sentence—an explanation being given in appropriate cases if other options have been considered and rejected.

Where custody is likely, the report should identify matters which might have adverse effects on the offender and his or her family, and any considerations relating to length of sentence.

CONFIDENTIALITY

Reports are confidential documents and the information in them is limited to what is relevant to the sentencing process. When a custodial sentence is passed, a copy is normally passed to the probation service/social services department in the custodial institution to assist in the sentence and release arrangements (see *Chapter 9*).

The content of the PSR is brought to the attention of the offender by the report writer. This may mean reading it out in private for those who cannot read; including having an interpreter read and translate it to an offender whose first language is not English. A copy of the PSR is given to the offender and to his or her legal representative.

PROVISIONAL INDICATIONS OF SERIOUSNESS

It assists the report writer in preparing a satisfactory PSR if a provisional view on seriousness is indicated by the court. This provides the report writer with a starting point. Conversely, it does not lead to the most effective analysis if the court merely announces that it wishes to keep all options open. Such vague statements became prevalent as a result of cases such as *R v Gillam* (1980) 2 Cr App R (S) 267 which held that if a court requests a report to ascertain eg the offender's suitability for community service, then if the report shows that the offender *is* suitable, the court should make the order—otherwise a feeling of injustice might arise. The court had created in the mind of those present the expectation of a non–custodial sentence.

Such problems can be overcome if a court makes a carefully worded pronouncement when requesting a PSR, eg:

> On what we have heard so far we feel that the offence is serious enough for a community sentence. We are, therefore, requesting a PSR to be prepared on that basis. However, nothing that we say today, or any suggestion in the report about how you should be dealt with, will prevent the court from taking a different view concerning the seriousness of the offence when it has considered all the information in the case.

If such an approach is followed, the report writer has a clear indication of the court's preliminary view, whilst the sentencing court is seemingly in no way restricted when it imposes sentence. This means that the court may, where appropriate, having considered *all* relevant information, decide to impose a custodial sentence or a fine or discharge as opposed to a community sentence.

NB It should be noted that courts approach this issue in differing ways and practices may vary. Magistrates should establish what the local arrangements are and, if necessary, seek legal advice.

STATEMENTS OF PREFERRED PRACTICE

Probation practice dictates that each probation area should develop a working agreement or statement of preferred practice with and for each magistrates' court in its area. Agreements are usually drawn up between the chairman of the bench and the justices' clerk and local probation service (in consultation with social services). Agreements may set time targets for the preparation of PSRs and afford priority to the situation where an offender is in custody awaiting sentence.

NATIONAL STANDARDS

'National Standards for the Supervision of Offenders in the Community' were first introduced by the Home Office, Welsh Office and Department of Health in 1992 and a revised version was published in 1995. HM Inspectorate of Probation measures satisfactory compliance with the standards. In relation to PSRs, a stated aim is to strengthen the service provided to courts by:

- building upon the skill and experience of practitioners
- enabling professional judgment to be exercised within a framework of accountability
- encouraging the adoption of good practice
- setting a priority on the protection of the public
- establishing the importance of considering the effect of crime on victims.

More generally, the standards set out what is required of probation staff and social workers, providing a framework for good practice, accountability and achievement.

RESPONDING TO A PSR

The PSR writer must consider the interests of the public as well as those of the offender. Sentencing is ultimately the responsibility of the court and there will be times when it declines to follow even a well reasoned PSR. There should be no need for any discord as between the court and the PSR writer if both have followed correct practice and proper procedures.

Chapter 9

The Early Release Scheme

A parole system has been in force in England and Wales since 1968. The Parole Board dealt with questions affecting the release of prisoners— and as a result of the then system of remission, prisoners (other than those serving a life sentence) were released from prison free from any restrictions after serving two–thirds of their sentence. It was also possible for an offender to be released on parole after serving one third of his or her sentence.

The system was in need of overhaul, partly because of the disparity between the sentence imposed and the actual time served. The Criminal Justice Act 1991 thus introduced the early release scheme described in this chapter. The new scheme—which is summarised in *Figure 3* on page 98—was based on proposals made in Lord Carlisle's report, *The Parole System in England and Wales: Report of the Review Committee* (1988, Cm 532).

Release on licence
All prisoners sentenced to imprisonment for 12 months or more are placed on licence on release until the three–quarters point of their sentence (though sex offenders may be on licence until the end of their sentence). Released prisoners are normally supervised by a probation officer as a condition of the licence (or if the person released on licence is under 22 years of age the supervisor can be a local authority social worker). The scheme applies equally to detention in a young offender institution.

Early release of short-term prisoners
Prisoners serving less than four years ('short term prisoners') must be released as soon as they have served one half of their sentence. If the sentence is for less than 12 months the prisoner is released *unconditionally* (ie not on licence)—usually referred to as 'automatic unconditional release' (AUR). If the sentence is for 12 months or more, but less than four years, the prisoner is released on licence subject to conditions—automatic conditional release (ACR).

In all cases, days lost for misbehaviour are added to the portion to be served before the offender is released.

Outline of the Early Release Scheme

- Prisoners serving less than 12 months are released automatically at the half-way stage of their sentence (sometimes called **AUTOMATIC UNCONDITIONAL RELEASE (AUR)**). They are eligible for voluntary after-care, and can be returned to prison by a court for the rest of the existing term (ie in addition to any prison sentence for the new offence) if they are convicted of a further imprisonable offence during this period.

- Prisoners serving 12 months to under four years are subject to **AUTOMATIC CONDITIONAL RELEASE (ACR)**

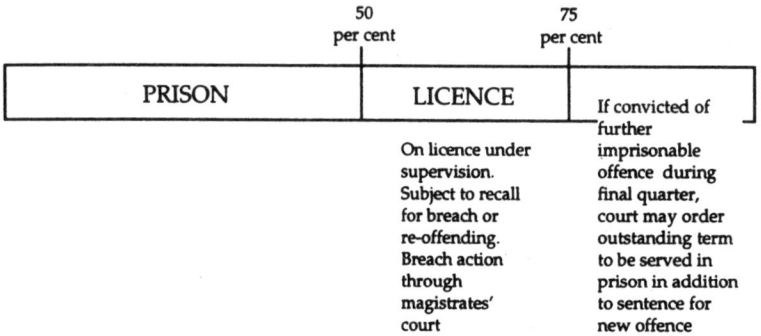

- Prisoners serving four years and above are subject to **DISCRETIONARY CONDITIONAL RELEASE (DCR)**

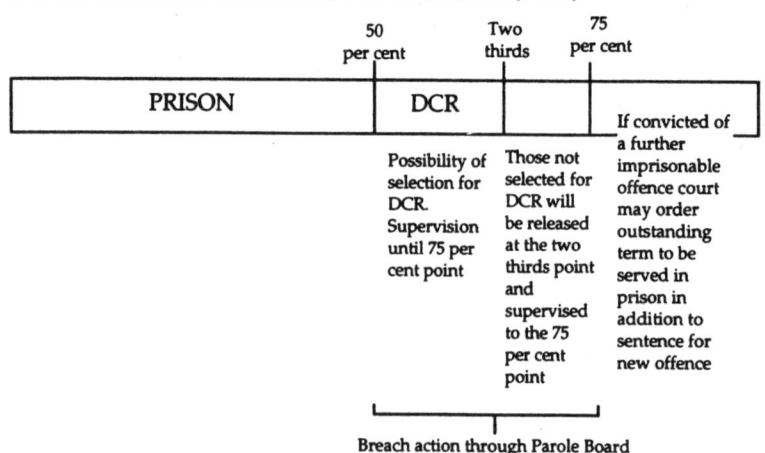

Figure 3

98

Early release of long-term prisoners
Prisoners serving four years or more must be released as soon as they have served two-thirds of their sentence, but can be released on licence at the half-way point—usually called 'discretionary conditional release' (DCR). In either case, the licence expires at the time when the prisoner would have served three-quarters of his or her sentence.

Days lost for misbehaviour are added to the portion to be served before the offender is released.

ENFORCEMENT

Enforcement has two main objectives:

- to secure compliance with the licence; and
- to recognise cases where this cannot be achieved and take action.

Throughout, the need to protect the public is a primary concern.

Breach of licence condition by short-term offenders
A short-term prisoner who fails to comply with the conditions of his or her ACR licence is liable on conviction in the magistrates' court to a fine not exceeding Level 3 (£1,000). In addition, the court may, whether or not it passes another sentence for a fresh offence, suspend the licence for a period not exceeding six months and order recall to prison for the period for which the licence is suspended. A pre-sentence report (PSR) is not required by law (but may be desirable in some instances). If not already in custody, the offender is liable to be detained and deemed to be unlawfully at large.

Breach of licence by long-term prisoners
The Home Secretary has power to revoke the licence and recall the offender to prison if recommended to do so by the Parole Board. If it appears expedient, the Home Secretary may do this without such a recommendation—but the Board must be informed.

Commission of a further offence
A court convicting a prisoner—long-term or short-term (including an AUR prisoner, released from a sentence of under 12 months)—of an imprisonable offence committed following early release but before the 'face value' of the original sentence has elapsed may, whether or not it passes a prison sentence for the new offence, order the offender to be

returned to prison for all or part of a period equal to whatever period of the original sentence remained on the day the offence was committed. The court has this power whether or not the conviction for the new offence occurs before or after the date on which he or she would have served the full sentence but for the early release. Magistrates' powers are limited to six months, but magistrates can commit to the Crown Court for sentence. The period can be ordered to be served before or concurrently with any sentence for the new offence. A PSR is not required (but may be desirable in some instances).

LICENCE CONDITIONS

Every licence contains standard conditions designed to facilitate its operation. Extra conditions may be imposed to prevent offending, ie:

- to attend upon a duly qualified psychiatrist, psychologist or medical practitioner for such care, supervision or treatment as that practitioner recommends
- not to engage in any work or other organized activity involving a person under a specified age
- to reside at a specified place and not to reside elsewhere without the prior approval of the supervising officer
- not to reside in the same household as any child under a given age
- not to approach or communicate with a specified person or persons without the prior approval of the supervising officer
- to comply with requirements imposed by the supervising officer to address problems relating to alcohol, drugs, gambling, sex offending, solvent abuse, anger, debt or offending generally.

Breach of any of these extra licence conditions has the effect already described above.

ROLE OF THE PROBATION SERVICE

The probation service works in co–operation with the prison service to carry out supervision of prisoners before and after release. The aims of this work are:

100

- protection of the public;
- prevention of re–offending; and
- successful reintegration into the community.

The work is governed by a 'National Standard for the Supervision of Offenders by the Probation Service Before and After Release'.

RESIDUAL PAROLE BOARD FUNCTIONS

Since 1991, the Parole Board plays a more limited role, principally in relation to long-term prisoners and 'lifers'. The Board advises the Home Secretary on matters referred to it which relate to the early release or recall of prisoners. The Board also deals with the discretionary conditional release (DCR) of offenders serving four years or more and also has powers to release a prisoner who is serving a discretionary life sentence (but not a mandatory life-sentence prisoner serving a term for murder, this being a matter for the Home Secretary to decide after considering a recommendation by the Board).

Chapter 10

Mental Disorder

In addition to its standard sentencing powers a magistrates' court has power to make the following orders:

- A hospital order whereby a person is detained for medical treatment until discharged.

- A guardianship order whereby a person is placed under the guardianship of a social services department or an approved person.

In every case the maximum possible sentence on conviction by magistrates must include imprisonment. The court need not have convicted the offender (because of problems over his or her mental state) but must be satisfied that the offender committed the act or omission alleged by the prosecution. The court must be in possession of medical reports from two doctors who are in agreement as to the offender's mental condition and be satisfied that any necessary arrangements for admission to hospital have been made.

Before such orders are made, a court may remand a person on bail, in custody, or, where appropriate, to a hospital for the necessary reports to be produced. Following reports being obtained, an interim hospital order may be made until the court is satisfied as to the correct disposal.

If a magistrates' court feels that there should be a restriction placed on the date of release from hospital, the court may commit the offender in custody to the Crown Court for an order restricting discharge to be attached to any hospital order made by that court.

The above matters are further explained later in the chapter.

DIVERSION FROM THE CRIMINAL PROCESS

Attempts are made to divert people away from the criminal courts if they are suffering from mental disorder and where treatment is considered to be more appropriate than punishment.

Many magistrates' courts are involved in such arrangements, which include duty psychiatrist schemes and multi–agency liaison to ensure that medical personnel are in attendance or on call. The arrangements stem from Home Office Circular 66/1990, 'Provision for Mentally Disordered Offenders'. The Crown Prosecution Service also endorses the spirit and objectives of the circular in its own Code of Practice.

INSANITY

If an accused person is brought before a court for a criminal offence, he or she may raise the defence of insanity. If this succeeds, he or she is liable to be detained at Her Majesty's pleasure, ie indefinitely. The defence is, therefore, in practice, confined to serious offences in the Crown Court where the consequences of conviction may be a very long sentence.

SENTENCING IN THE ORDINARY WAY

If a mentally disordered person is capable of being dealt with by the court and is found guilty, all normal sentencing options apply, including a probation order with a condition of medical or psychiatric treatment: see *Chapter 3*. Mentally disturbed offenders cannot be committed to prison simply because of their mental condition—ordinary sentencing principles apply as with every other defendant. However, if a court is considering custody for a mentally disordered offender, the law obliges it to obtain a psychiatric report before making that a decision.

SPECIAL PROVISIONS

The law gives the courts special sentencing powers where a defendant pleads guilty or is found guilty of an offence—for which the maximum penalty on conviction by magistrates includes imprisonment—and where he or she is in need of psychiatric treatment and suffering from one of four categories of mental disorder defined in the Mental Health Act 1983. The orders in question are hospital orders and guardianship orders: see below.

Orders made without a conviction
If magistrates are satisfied that the accused did the act or made the omission charged, they may, in the circumstances described below, make a hospital or guardianship order *without* convicting the accused.

Even if the offence is triable either way (see *Chapter 1*) and the accused is unable, because of his or her mental condition, to consent to summary trial the same procedure applies and an order may be made. The circumstances referred to above are as follows:

- The court must first be satisfied that the offender did the act or made the omission with which he or she is charged, ie the physical element of the offence (known as the *actus reus*) as opposed to the mental element (*mens rea*)
- The court must be satisfied on the written or oral evidence of two registered medical practitioners (one of whom must be approved for the purpose) that the offender is suffering from mental illness, or psychopathic disorder, severe mental impairment or mental impairment as defined in the Mental Health Act 1983. This will be by a psychiatrist (but note that both psychiatrists and chartered psychologists can provide treatment under probation orders)
- The court must be of the opinion, having regard to all the circumstances, including the offence, antecedents, and other available methods of disposal, that the most appropriate method of disposal is the order under consideration.
- When making a hospital order, the court must be satisfied on oral or written evidence that arrangements have been made for the offender to be admitted to a specified hospital within 28 days.

HOSPITAL ORDERS

The effect of a hospital order is that the offender is admitted to hospital and detained there—initially for 12 months or until discharged by the hospital authorities or a Mental Health Review Tribunal. The court may give directions for the offender to be detained in a suitable place until he or she can be admitted to the hospital.

Courts have sometimes experienced difficulty when arranging for mentally disordered offenders to be admitted to hospital—either for a full hospital order or an interim hospital order (below). One reason for this has been the large increase in demand for what the Department of Health calls 'medium secure beds'—brought about by the substantial increase in the number of prisoners transferred to hospital under Mental Health Act provisions. There is planned development within the National Health Service capital programme to provide further beds. In the meantime, a named senior officer in each Regional Health Authority can be contacted by telephone—the aim being to assist the court by finding an appropriate placement as expeditiously as possible.

Orders restricting discharge

Where the Crown Court makes a hospital order, that court may also make a restriction order if this is considered necessary for the protection of the public. The order restricts release for a specified, or indefinite, period. In practice, restriction orders are for more serious offences—and cannot be made by magistrates' courts.

If magistrates consider that the accused is likely to commit further offences if at large, then having regard to the nature of the offence and the antecedents of the offender, they may commit him or her in custody to the Crown Court for a restriction order to be made.

Interim hospital orders

If a hospital order might be appropriate the court has power to make an interim hospital order, ie where it is not sure whether to make a full order straight away or deal with the offender in some other way.

Before making an interim order the court must be satisfied that all necessary arrangements have been made for admission to the hospital (in this situation *within* 28 days). Interim orders last for a maximum period of six months. At the end of the period of the interim order the court may make a full hospital order or deal with the offender in some other way.

GUARDIANSHIP ORDERS

Guardianship orders place the offender under the guardianship of a local authority social services department or of some person approved by the local authority. The purpose of such an order is to enable patients to receive community care where it cannot be provided without the use of compulsory powers. Someone who is subject to a guardianship order is not liable to be detained. Treatment cannot be given without consent.

Guardianship orders may be particularly suitable in helping to meet the needs of mentally impaired offenders who could benefit from occupation, training and education in the community.

The pre–conditions for making guardianship orders are essentially the same as for hospital orders (above). Orders remain in force for an initial period of six months but may be renewed. The effect of such an order is to give the guardian power to require the patient to live at a specified place, to attend places at specified times for medical treatment, occupation, education or training and to allow access by a doctor, approved social worker or other specified persons.

REPORTS

Before making either a hospital order or guardianship order the court must receive and consider appropriate reports (including, where applicable, a PSR) and be satisfied, in the case of a hospital order, that the necessary arrangements have been made for admission. In addition to its ordinary powers to remand on bail or in custody the court has two further powers: to remand the offender to a hospital for a report on his mental condition if the court is satisfied by written or oral evidence that arrangements have been made for admission to a specified hospital within seven days; or to make interim orders (above).

In summary:

- the defendant must be remanded (ie kept in custody for up to three weeks or released on bail for up to four weeks)
- conditions attached to bail can ensure co-operation with the preparation of reports
- if the offender is in custody, the prison will arrange for the reports
- if the offender is on bail, the court (often with the help of a probation officer, who will usually be requested to write a co-ordinated PSR) will make the arrangements
- only a 'duly qualified medical practitioner' can prepare the report
- special scales of fees are paid by courts for reports.

Mental disorder is a complex subject and it is essential that defendants are legally represented whenever possible. Equally, it is advisable for magistrates to seek legal advice. The outline provided in this chapter represents no more than a basic introduction, sufficient to familiarise readers with the core issues.

Chapter 11

The Role of the Legal Advisor

Sentencing has become more complex in recent times, due mainly to an increasing amount of legislation. This has created a range of new offences and introduced fresh rules, procedures and sentencing considerations. Whilst the sentence of the court now takes place within the framework outlined in this handbook, there are often further legal considerations. Courts are also required to give valid reasons or explanations for a range of sentence-related decisions.

LAW, PRACTICE AND PROCEDURE

The law in relation to sentencing is found not only in Acts of Parliament and Statutory Instruments (SIs), but also in rulings of the Court of Appeal (Criminal Division) and the High Court. These courts interpret sentencing legislation and occasionally give general guidance.

The Court of Appeal has emphasised that its decisions in relation to appeals against sentence—see the examples of case summaries on page 59—serve as examples of how a particular offender ought to have been dealt with in relation to a given offence. What are known as 'Guideline judgments'—ie rulings which deal with sentencing issues in a more general way—are clearly of greater import than an isolated appeal ruling. Many rulings of the higher courts are reported in 'law reports', whilst any significant developments are noted in the legal journals.

In addition, non-binding guidance on a range of matters is issued by Ministers of the Crown acting within their particular fields of responsibility. Thus, the Home Secretary is responsible for criminal policy, including the development of legislation affecting the sentences available to the courts. Home Office circulars—issued to courts and others—outline the official stance.

The practice in an area or locality is also something which affects the way in which sentence decisions are arrived at.

It is the responsibility of the court legal advisor to be familiar with all these items—and particularly with current developments. All advisors are professionals who receive special training in this regard. Their specialities include evidence, procedure and sentencing.

THE JUSTICES' CLERK

The justices' clerk—as the legal advisor to the bench—is under a duty to ensure that justices receive all appropriate legal advice. The justices' clerk's duties (which may be discharged on a day-to-day basis by other legal staff) are set out in statute and augmented in a *Practice Direction* issued by Lord Lane when Lord Chief Justice. The relevant parts of the direction are reproduced below.

The main duties of the justices' clerk and other legal advisors are to advise magistrates on matters relating to law, practice and procedure. The relevant statutory provision states

> . . . it is hereby declared that the functions of a justices' clerk include the giving to the justices to whom he is clerk, or any of them, at the request of the justices or justice, advice about law, practice or procedure . . . including questions arising when the clerk is not personally attending on the justices or justice and the clerk may, at any time when he thinks he should do so, bring to the attention of the justices or justice any point of law, practice or procedure that is or may be involved in any question so arising.

The independent nature of this duty is reinforced by the Police and Magistrates' Courts Act 1994 under which the justices' clerk and his or her staff are protected, in individual cases, from any form of direction, from whatever source, when carrying out their responsibilities.

The Practice Direction

The role of the justices' clerk/legal advisor is nowhere better encapsulated than in the *Practice Direction* given by Lord Lane in 1981:

Magistrates' Courts—The Role of the Clerk

> **1.** A justices' clerk is responsible to the justices for the performance of any of the functions set out below by any member of his staff acting as court clerk and may be called in to advise the justices even when he is not personally sitting with the justices as clerk to the court.
>
> **2.** It shall be the responsibility of the justices' clerk to advise the justices as follows:
>
> [a] on questions of law or of mixed law and fact;
> [b] as to matters of practice and procedure
>
> **3.** If it appears to him necessary to do so, or he is so requested by the justices, the justices' clerk has the responsibility to:
>
> [a] refresh the justices' memory as to any matter of evidence and to draw attention to any issues involved in the matters before the court;

[b] advise the justices generally on the range of penalties which the law allows them to impose and on any guidance relevant to the choice of penalty provided by the law, the decisions of the superior courts or other authorities.

If no request for advice has been made by the justices, the justices' clerk shall discharge his responsibility in court in the presence of the parties.

4. The way in which a justices' clerk should perform his functions should be stated as follows:

[a] the justices are entitled to the advice of their clerk when they retire in order that the clerk may fulfil his responsibility outlined above.
[b] Some justices may prefer to take their own notes of evidence. There is, however, no obligation upon them to do so. Whether they do so or not, there is nothing to prevent them from enlisting the aid of their clerk and his notes if they are in doubt as to the evidence which has been given.
[c] If the justices wish to consult their clerk solely about the evidence or his notes of it, this should ordinarily, and certainly in simple cases, be done in open court. The object is to avoid any suspicion that the clerk has been involved in deciding issues of fact.

The *Practice Direction* thus places a responsibility on the legal advisor to advise magistrates on any guidance relevant to the choice of penalty provided by the law and the decisions of the higher courts or other authorities. This includes the sentencing principles laid down by the Court of Appeal (above). A previous *Practice Direction* also indicated that it may be appropriate for the clerk to give information about sentences already imposed by the bench, or by neighbouring benches, in respect of similar offences to those being tried by the justices—since it is desirable to achieve uniformity of approach whenever possible.

In the retiring room
When justices adjourn to their private quarters to consider sentence it is good practice—whenever there are matters within the ambit of the *Practice Direction* and in all but the most straightforward cases—to consider seeking legal advice at some stage. In some instances this will need to be at the outset. However, the legal advisor should not retire with the magistrates as a matter of course (nor where the decision is a straightforward one which does not involve any legal or other considerations within the responsibility of the advisor) and, if they do require advice, he or she should be audibly invited to join them.

If not sent for, the advisor is still entitled to go to the magistrates and to give them such advice as seems necessary—but he or she should inform the parties as to what is going to be said. Where the advisor has discussions with the justices after they have returned from retirement and the result is that they wish to retire again and on this occasion take the advisor with them, the parties should receive an explanation.

In practice, advice is often given in open court and in the hearing of the parties—as envisaged by the *Practice Direction*. Where this is not the case, it is good practice for the parties to receive some explanation and, if appropriate, to be given the chance to make further representations before the court makes a final decision.

Personal liability

Justices have been warned by Lord Taylor, Lord Chief Justice, that if they fail to take appropriate advice on a settled legal point they could be held personally liable for the costs of any appeal. The case in question concerned an everday matter, ie whether 'special reasons' for endorsing a driving licence could be found (*Chapter 7*) and salient advice—which was wrongly rejected—had been given both verbally and in writing.

Appendix A National Mode of Trial Guidelines

Foreword

The National Mode of Trial Guidelines were produced in October 1990. They have proved extremely useful and helpful to magistrates having to decide whether or not to commit 'either way' offences to the Crown Court for trial. Now, they have been revised and brought up to date by the Secretariat of the Criminal Justice Consultative Council. The Secretariat and all those who have assisted them, from the Home Office, the Lord Chancellor's Department, the Law Officers Department, the Crown Prosecution Service, the Magistrates' Association and the Justices' Clerks are to be congratulated and thanked for their work.

It must be recognised that in this field as in others, guidelines are offered by way of assistance not as directions. That said, those who have the difficult decisions to make on Mode of Trial will find these revised guidelines most helpful. I commend them wholeheartedly.

(Signed) Taylor CJ
Lord Chief Justice of England

National Mode of Trial Guidelines 1995

The purpose of these guidelines is to help magistrates decide whether or not to commit 'either way' offences for trial in the Crown Court. Their object is to provide guidance not direction. They are not intended to impinge upon a magistrate's duty to consider each case individually and on its own particular facts.

These guidelines apply to all defendants **aged 18 and above.**

General Mode of Trial Considerations

Section 19 of the Magistrates' Court Act 1980 requires magistrates to have regard to the following matters in deciding whether an offence is more suitable for summary trial or trial on indictment:

1. the nature of the case
2. whether the circumstances make the offence one of a serious character
3. whether the punishment which a magistrates' court would have power to inflict for it would be adequate
4. any other circumstances which appear to the court to make it more suitable for the offence to be tried in one way rather than the other
5. any representations made by the prosecution or the defence.

Certain general observations can be made:

a. the court should never make its decision on the grounds of convenience or expedition

b. the court should assume for the purpose of deciding mode of trial that the prosecution version of the facts is correct

c. the fact that the offences are alleged to be specimens is a relevant consideration; the fact that the defendant will be asking for other offences to be taken into consideration, if convicted, is not

d. where cases involve complex questions of fact or difficult questions of law, including difficult issues of disclosure of sensitive material, the court should consider committal for trial

e. where two or more defendants are jointly charged with an offence each has an individual right to elect his mode of trial. [This follows the decision in *R v Brentwood Justices ex parte Nicholls.*]

f. *In general, except where otherwise stated, either way offences should be tried summarily unless the court considers that the particular case has one or more of the features set out in the following pages and that its sentencing powers are insufficient.*

g. The court should also consider its power to commit an offender for sentence, under Section 38 of the Magistrates' Courts Act 1980, as amended by Section 25 of the Criminal Justice Act 1991, **if information emerges during the course of the hearing which leads them to conclude that the offence is so serious, or the offender such a risk to the public, that their powers to sentence him are inadequate.** This amendment means that committal for sentence is no longer determined by reference to the character or antecedents of the defendant.

Features relevant to the individual offences

Note: Where reference is made in these guidelines to property or damage of **'high value'** it means a figure equal to at least **twice** the amount of the limit (currently £5,000) imposed by statute on a magistrates' court when making a compensation order.

Burglary

Cases should be tried summarily unless the court considers that one or more of the following features is present in the case and that its sentencing powers are insufficient.

Magistrates should take account of their powers under S25 of the Criminal Justice Act 1991 to commit for **sentence**.

Note: See paragraph (g) on page [112].

1. Dwelling House

1. Entry in the daytime when the occupier (or another) is present
2. Entry at night of a house which is normally occupied, whether or not the occupier (or another) is present
3. The offence is alleged to be one of a series of similar offences
4. When soiling, ransacking, damage or vandalism occurs
5. The offence has professional hallmarks
6. The unrecovered property is of high value (see page [112] for definition of high value)

Note: Attention is drawn to para 28(c) of Schedule 1 of the Magistrates' Courts Act 1980, by which offences of burglary in a dwelling **cannot** be tried summarily if any person in the dwelling was subjected to violence or the threat of violence.

Burglary

Cases should be tried summarily unless the court considers that one or more of the following features is present in the case and that its sentencing powers are insufficient.

Magistrates should take account of their powers under S25 of the Criminal Justice Act 1991 to commit for **sentence**.

Note: See paragraph (g) on page [112].

2. Non-Dwellings

1. Entry of a pharmacy or doctor's surgery
2. Fear is caused or violence is done to anyone lawfully on the premises (eg nightwatchman; security guard)
3. The offence has professional hallmarks
4. Vandalism on a substantial scale
5. The unrecovered property is of high value (see page [112] for definition of high value)

Theft and Fraud

Cases should be tried summarily unless the court considers that one or more of the following features is present in the case and that its sentencing powers are insufficient.

Magistrates should take account of their powers under S25 of the Criminal Justice Act 1991 to commit for **sentence**.

Note: See paragraph (g) on page [112].

1. Breach of trust by a person in a position of substantial authority, or in whom a high degree of trust is placed

113

2. Theft or fraud which has been committed or disguised in a sophisticated manner
3. Theft or fraud committed by an organised gang
4. The victim is particularly vulnerable to theft or fraud eg the elderly or infirm
5. The unrecovered property is of high value (see page [112] for definition of high value)

Handling

Cases should be tried summarily unless the court considers that one or more of the following features is present in the case and that its sentencing powers are insufficient.

Magistrates should take account of their powers under S25 of the Criminal Justice Act 1991 to commit for **sentence.**

Note: See paragraph (g) on page [112].

1. Dishonest handling of stolen property by a receiver who has commissioned the theft
2. The offence has professional hallmarks
3. The property is of high value (see page 3 for definition of high value)

Social Security Frauds

Cases should be tried summarily unless the court considers that one or more of the following features is present in the case and that its sentencing powers are insufficient.

Magistrates should take account of their powers under S25 of the Criminal Justice Act 1991 to commit for **sentence.**

Note: See paragraph (g) on page [112].

1. Organised fraud on a large scale
2. The frauds are substantial and carried out over a long period of time

Violence (Sections 20 and 47 of the Offences Against the Person Act 1861)

Cases should be tried summarily unless the court considers that one or more of the following features is present in the case and that its sentencing powers are insufficient.

Magistrates should take account of their powers under S25 of the Criminal Justice Act 1991 to commit for **sentence.**

Note: See paragraph (g) on page [112].

1. The use of a weapon of a kind likely to cause serious injury
2. A weapon is used and serious injury is caused
3. More than minor injury is caused by kicking, head butting or similar forms of assault
4. Serious violence is caused to those whose work has to be done in contact with the public or who are likely to face violence in the course of their work
5. Violence to vulnerable people eg the elderly and infirm
6. The offence has clear racial motivation

Note: The same considerations apply to cases **of domestic** violence.

Public Order Act Offences

Cases should be tried summarily unless the court considers that one or more of the following features is present in the case and that its sentencing powers are insufficient.

Magistrates should take account of their powers under S25 of the Criminal Justice Act 1991 to commit for **sentence.**

Note: See paragraph (g) on page [112].

1. Cases of **Violent Disorder** should generally be committed for trial

2. Affray
1. Organised violence or use of weapons
2. Significant injury or substantial damage
3. The offence has clear racial motivation
4. An attack upon police officers, prison officers, ambulance men, firemen and the like

Violence To and Neglect Of Children

Cases should be tried summarily unless the court considers that one or more of the following features is present in the case and that its sentencing powers are insufficient.

Magistrates should take account of their powers under S25 of the Criminal Justice Act 1991 to commit for **sentence.**

Note: See paragraph (g) on page [112].

1. Substantial injury
2. Repeated violence or serious neglect, even if the physical harm is slight
3. Sadistic violence eg deliberate burning or scalding

Indecent Assault

Cases should be tried summarily unless the court considers that one or more of the following features is present in the case and that its sentencing powers are insufficient.

Magistrates should take account of their powers under S25 of the Criminal Justice Act 1991 to commit for **sentence.**

Note: See paragraph (g) on page [112].

1. Substantial disparity in age between victim and defendant, and the assault is more than trivial
2. Violence or threats of violence
3. Relationship of trust or responsibility between defendant and victim
4. Several similar offences, and the assaults are more than trivial
5. The victim is particularly vulnerable
6. Serious nature of the assault

Unlawful Sexual Intercourse

Cases should be tried summarily unless the court considers that one or more of the following features is present in the case and that its sentencing powers are insufficient.

Magistrates should take account of their powers under S25 of the Criminal Justice Act 1991 to commit for **sentence.**

Note: See paragraph (g) on page [112].

1. Wide disparity of age
2. Breach of position of trust
3. The victim is particularly vulnerable

Drugs

1. Class A

    a.   Supply; possession with intent to supply
        These cases should be committed for trial

    b.   Possession
        Should be committed for trial unless the amount is consistent only with personal use

2. Class B

    a.   Supply; possession with intent to supply
        Should be committed for trial unless there is only small scale supply for no payment

    b.   Possession
        Should be committed for trial when the quantity is substantial and not consistent only with personal use

Dangerous Driving

Cases should be tried summarily unless the court considers that one or more of the following features is present in the case and that its sentencing powers are insufficient.

Magistrates should take account of their powers under S25 of the Criminal Justice Act 1991 to commit for **sentence.**

Note: See paragraph (g) on page [112].

1. Alcohol or drugs contributing to dangerousness
2. Grossly excessive speed
3. Racing
4. Prolonged course of dangerous driving
5. Degree of injury or damage sustained
6. Other related offences

Criminal Damage

Cases should be tried summarily unless the court considers that one or more of the following features is present in the case and that its sentencing powers are insufficient.

Magistrates should take account of their powers under S25 of the Criminal Justice Act 1991 to commit for **sentence.**

Note: See paragraph (g) on page [112].

1. Deliberate fire-raising
2. Committed by group
3 Damage of a high value
4. The offence has clear racial motivation

Note: Offences set out in Schedule 2 of the Magistrates' Courts Act 1980 (which includes offences of criminal damage which do not amount to arson) must be tried summarily if the value of the property damaged or destroyed is £5,000 or less.

Appendix B

Magistrates' Association
Sentencing Guidelines

Reproduced by kind permission of the Association

This edition of the Magistrates' Association Sentencing Guidelines has been produced in consultation with Stipendiary Magistrates and the Justices' Clerks' Society. Grateful thanks go to all those involved in this unique collaboration.

The Sentencing Guidelines are issued with the blessing of the Lord Chancellor and the Lord Chief Justice. The Guidelines are endorsed by the Justices' Clerks' Society.

Mrs J D H Rose
Chairman of Council

© The Magistrates' Association September 1993

THE
MAGISTRATES'
ASSOCIATION

118

SENTENCING
GUIDELINES

CONTENTS

Introduction and User Guide

This guide deals with criminal offences which come before magistrates' courts frequently. A structure is provided to suggest:—

— how to assess the relative seriousness of each case, and
— how to arrive at a commensurate penalty

Magistrates should always remember that the guidelines are only starting points for discussion of individual sentences. The guide gives a number of entry points for thinking and discussion. The guidelines deal with offenders of 18 years of age and over.

Entry Points

For all types of case, including road traffic cases, the guide provides entry points, not finishing points. The term 'entry point' has been used to give a guide for an offence of 'average' seriousness. Justices will have to consider whether the particular case before them is of average seriousness or whether there are specific aggravating or mitigating circumstances which make it more serious or less serious than the average offence of that type. Having considered the seriousness of the offence, the justices will have to consider any personal mitigating factors and decide whether any such factor(s) enable them to change the kind of penalty which the offence would otherwise merit.

The responsibility for the sentence is that of the justices and it is they who must assess each case judicially having regard to (a) the circumstances of the particular offence and (b) the circumstances of the particular offender.

Where the entry point is a fine the guideline fine is that which is regarded as appropriate for an offence of average seriousness. It follows that the bench when considering an individual case will have to decide whether there are particular features of the case which either aggravate or mitigate the seriousness of the offence and, if there are, they will have to decide whether a fine is appropriate and, if it is, whether the level of the fine should be above or below the guideline. Having considered the seriousness of the offence the Bench will then have to consider any personal mitigation and, assuming that a fine s still the appropriate penalty, they must then consider the offender's means. If of below average means, the amount should be reduced to a level which the offender can realistically be expected to pay and, if of above average means, there is a presumption that the fine should be increased.

The guideline sentences represent a broad consensus of view and are based on a first-time offender pleading not-guilty. A timely guilty plea may be regarded as a mitigating factor for which a sentencing discount of approximately one-third might be given. The precise discount a court should allow must depend upon the facts of the case. An early admission of guilt where an offence would otherwise be undetected should attract a substantial discount; on the other hand, a last minute guilty plea when faced with witnesses may attract only a nominal discount. The existence of relevant previous offences and/or failures to respond to previous sentences may be regarded as aggravating factors.

Means forms

The means form is no longer a statutory requirement but before fixing the amount of any fine the court must enquire into the financial circumstances of the offender. If there is insufficient information to make a proper determination, the court may make such determination as it thinks fit.

The Association is aware that there are many local means forms in existence and suggests that courts build on these. However, as a general guide means forms should be as simple to complete as possible and in line with a broad approach to income and other financial resources. In order to encourage defendants to complete the means form, it is suggested that the form carries a simple warning, for example:

IF YOU DO NOT FILL IN THE FORM YOU MAY BE FINED MORE HEAVILY THAN YOU CAN AFFORD

Penalties

The fine imposed is determined by the court to be commensurate with the seriousness of the offence(s) before the court. The amount of the fine shall not exceed the upper limit for the level of offence ie:—

For a level 1 offence — £200
For a level 2 offence — £500
For a level 3 offence — £1000
For a level 4 offence — £2500
For a level 5 offence — £5000

The offence

Each page deals with a separate offence. The process is:—

How serious is the case compared with other offences of this type?

— Consider the various 'seriousness indicators'
— Remember that these lists are not comprehensive and other factors may be important in individual cases
— Previous convictions or failure to respond to previous sentences may be taken into account in considering the seriousness of the present offence. It is recommended that courts should clearly identify which convictions or failures are relevant for this purpose and then consider what the effect of such convictions or failures is in relation to seriousness.
— Consider all aggravating or mitigating factors. Remember that the fact that an offence was committed whilst the offender was on bail should be treated as an aggravating factor.

Note that when there are several offences, the overall sentence should be kept in proportion to the totality of the offending behaviour with which the court is dealing

If in any doubt seek advice from the clerk.

Mode of trial

If the offence is triable either way, the seriousness indicators are relevant to the mode of trial decision but see the National Mode of Trial Guidelines which provide more comprehensive information (available from the Lord Chancellor's Department)

The offender

After assessing the seriousness of the offence, the court should then consider any mitigating factors relating to the offender (eg. age. health, co-operation with the police, voluntary compensation, guilty plea or remorse).

Sentencing framework

The fine is the penalty most frequently imposed by magistrates' court. However it must be recognised that many factors hinder consistency, in particular the duty to give priority to compensation may lead to an apparently lenient fine for a defendant on a low income.

The progression, based on seriousness, is as follows:—

— Consider discharge
— Consider compensation order alone or with other penalties
— Consider compensation and/or fine
— If serious enough consider a community penalty (ie. an attendance centre order (12-36 hours) , a community service order (40-240 hours unpaid work), a probation order (6 months- 3 years. with or without requirements), or a combination order (1-3 years probation plus 40-100 hours community service))
— If too serious for a community penalty consider custody
— If custody is justified, decide on length of sentence
— If significantly greater punishment than 6 months is appropriate, commit for sentence

Note: Whichever sentence is selected, custody and community penalties must be commensurate with the seriousness of the offence and fines must reflect seriousness. The one exception is where 'protection of the public from serious harm' is involved for violent or sexual offences only, which will usually be a reason for committing to the Crown Court for sentence. If in any doubt seek advice from the clerk.

Compensation should always be considered, even where custody is used. It should be awarded only in clear, simple, uncomplicated cases, otherwise consult the clerk. Further guidance is given at page 7.

Custody and community penalties

The law requires the court to take certain information into account before deciding on sentence. There must be a pre-sentence report in relation to custody and most forms of community penalty. Custody can only be used when the offence is so serious that no other sentence is justified. Community penalties can only be used where the offence is serious enough. When considering particular community penalties rehabilitation is a proper consideration in relation to probation orders and the probation part of a combination order.

The restrictions on liberty imposed by the sentence chosen must be commensurate with seriousness and the sentence must be the most suitable for the offender.

The justices' clerk/court clerk

Sentencing is a complex field and the justices' clerk or court clerk must advise the bench on the maximum penalties and powers available and assist as to the nature of the options and statutory restrictions, especially those relating to custodial sentences.

A Practice Direction states that

'If it appears to him necessary to do so, or he is requested by the justices, the justices' clerk has the responsibility to....advise the justices generally on the range of penalties which the law allows them to impose and on any guidance relevant to the decisions of the superior courts and other authorities.'

Compensation Orders

Priorities

Compensation is an order in its own right, and should be treated as such — particularly where the offender has insufficient means to pay a fine as well.

Damages

Where compensation is to be awarded for damage to, for example, a window, the cost must be proved or agreed.

Payment by instalments

An order for compensation should normally be payable within 12 months, but this can be exceeded up to a three year limit where the circumstances justify it.

Giving reasons

Section 35, Powers of the Criminal Courts Act 1973 states that

'A court shall give reasons on passing sentence if it does not make (a compensation) order in a case where this section empowers it to do so'.

Powers and limitations

Magistrates have power to award compensation for personal injury loss or damage up to a total of £5,000 for each offence. The compensation may relate to offences taken into consideration. There are exceptions including injury, loss or damage due to a road accident unless the damage results from an offence under the Theft Act 1968 or the offender is uninsured and the Motor Insurers Bureau will not cover the loss - if in any doubt, seek advice from the clerk.

An order for compensation should be considered whether or not there is an application by or on behalf of the victim. An award in the magistrates' court will not preclude a civil claim. 'Personal injury' need not be a physical injury. An award can be made, eg. for terror or distress caused by the offence.

Criminal Injuries Compensation Board

The Criminal Injuries Compensation Scheme is intended to compensate victims of violent crime and particularly those who are seriously injured. The minimum award s currently £1,000. Courts are encouraged to order offenders to compensate the victim whether or not the injury comes within the scope of the Criminal Injuries Compensation Scheme in order to bring home to offenders the personal consequences of their actions. To prevent double compensation for the same injury the Scheme provides for an award to be reduced by the amount of any compensation previously ordered by a criminal court.

Suggested compensation

Damages are assessed under two main headings — general damages, which is compensation for the pain and suffering of the injury itself and for any loss of facility; and special damages, which is compensation for financial loss sustained as a result of the injury — eg. loss of earnings, dental expenses etc. The suggestions given in the table below are for general damages.

The following guidelines are taken from the Home Office Draft Circular issued in August 1993.

The figures below are only a very general guide and may be increased or decreased according to the medical evidence, the victim's sex, age and any other factors which appear to the court to be relevant in the particular case. If the court does not have enough information to make a decision, then the matter should be adjourned to obtain more facts.

TYPE OF INJURY		SUGGESTED AWARD
Graze	depending on size	up to £50
Bruise	depending on size	up to £75
Black eye		£100
Cut: no permanent scarring	depending on size and whether stitched	£75-£500
Sprain	depending on loss of mobility	£100-£1,000
Loss of a non-front tooth	depending on cosmetic effect and age of victim	£250-£500
Other minor injury	causing reasonable absence from work (2-3) weeks	£550-£850
Loss of a front tooth		£1,000
Facial scar	however small - resulting in permanent disfigurement	£750+
Jaw	fractured (wired)	£2,750
Nasal	undisplaced fracture of the nasal bone	£750
Nasal	displaced fracture of bone requiring manipulation	£1,000
Nasal	not causing fracture but displaced septum requiring sub-mucous resection	£1,750
Wrist	simple fracture with complete recovery in few weeks	£1,750-£2,500
Wrist	displaced fracture - limb in plaster for some 6 weeks; full recovery 6-12 months	£2,500+
Finger	fractured little finger; assuming full recovery after a few weeks	£750
Leg or arm	simple fracture of tibia, fibula, ulna or radius with full recovery in three weeks	£2,500
Laparotomy	stomach scar 6-8 inches long (resulting from exploratory operation)	£3,500

Triable either way - see Mode of Trial Guidelines

Penalty: Level 5 and/or 6 months.

| ENTRY POINT | / | FINE | (−) |

(+) **CONSIDER THE SERIOUSNESS OF THE OFFENCE**

eg.
Short period

eg.
Offence committed on bail
High usage
Prolonged period
Special equipment
Previous convictions and failures to respond
to previous sentences, if relevant

IS COMPENSATION, DISCHARGE OR FINE APPROPRIATE?
IS IT SERIOUS ENOUGH FOR A COMMUNITY PENALTY?
IS IT SO SERIOUS THAT ONLY CUSTODY IS APPROPRIATE?

CONSIDER OFFENDER MITIGATION

eg.
Guilty plea: *for a timely guilty plea allow a discount of about a third*
Age, health (physical or mental)
Co-operation with the police
Voluntary compensation
Remorse

DECIDE YOUR SENTENCE

Compare your decision with the entry point - FINE - and check your reasons if you have
reached a different sentence

Guideline fine for this offence is £270 which reflects the average seriousness of an offence of
this type

NB. COMPENSATION - Give reasons if not awarding compensation
NB. FINES - If imposing a fine, remember to increase or decrease the amount according to the
financial circumstances of the offender

Triable either way - see Mode of Trial Guidelines

Penalty: Level 5 and/or 6 months

| ENTRY POINT | / | COMMUNITY PENALTY | (−) |

(+) **CONSIDER THE SERIOUSNESS OF THE OFFENCE**

eg.
Single offender

eg.
Offence committed on bail
Busy public place
Group action
People put in fear
Vulnerable victim(s)
Previous convictions and failures to respond
to previous sentences, if relevant

IS IT SERIOUS ENOUGH FOR A COMMUNITY PENALTY?
IS COMPENSATION, DISCHARGE OR FINE APPROPRIATE, OR
IS IT SO SERIOUS THAT ONLY CUSTODY IS APPROPRIATE?

CONSIDER OFFENDER MITIGATION

eg.
Guilty plea: *for a timely guilty plea allow a discount of about a third*
Age, health (physical or mental)
Co-operation with the police
Voluntary compensation
Remorse

DECIDE YOUR SENTENCE

Compare your decision with the entry point - COMMUNITY PENALTY - and check your
reasons if you have reached a different sentence

NB. COMPENSATION - Give reasons if not awarding compensation
NB. FINES - If imposing a fine, remember to increase or decrease the amount according to the
financial circumstances of the offender

Assault — Actual Bodily Harm

Offences Against the Person Act 1861 s.47
Triable either way - see Mode of Trial Guidelines
Penalty: Level 5 and/or 6 months

ENTRY POINT ✓	COMMUNITY PENALTY

CONSIDER THE SERIOUSNESS OF THE OFFENCE

eg.

	eg.
Offence committed on bail	Impulsive action
Deliberate kicking	Minor injury
Extensive injuries	Provocation
Group action	
Offender in position of authority	
Premeditated	
Victim particularly vulnerable	
Victim serving public	
Weapon	
Previous convictions and failures to respond to previous sentences, if relevant	

> IS IT SERIOUS ENOUGH FOR A COMMUNITY PENALTY?
> IS IT COMPENSATION, DISCHARGE OR FINE APPROPRIATE, OR
> IS IT SO SERIOUS THAT ONLY CUSTODY IS APPROPRIATE?

CONSIDER OFFENDER MITIGATION

eg.
Guilty plea: *for a timely guilty plea allow a discount of about a third*
Age, health (physical or mental)
Co-operation with the police
Voluntary compensation
Remorse

DECIDE YOUR SENTENCE

Compare your decision with the entry point - COMMUNITY PENALTY - and check your reasons if you have reached a different sentence

NB. COMPENSATION - Give reasons if not awarding compensation
NB. FINES - If imposing a fine, remember to increase or decrease the amount according to the financial circumstances of the offender

---

Aggravated Vehicle-Taking

Theft Act 1968 s. 12A as inserted by
Aggravated Vehicle-Taking Act 1992
Triable either way - but in certain cases summarily only - consult clerk.
Penalty: Level 5 and/or 6 months
Must endorse and disqualify at least 12 months:
Must endorse (3-11 points) if not disqualified

ENTRY POINT ✓	CUSTODY

CONSIDER THE SERIOUSNESS OF THE OFFENCE

eg.

	eg.
Offence committed on bail	Keys left in car
Avoiding detection or apprehension	No alcohol or drugs involved
Competitive driving; racing, showing off	Minor damage
Disregard of warnings eg from passengers or others in vicinity	Single incident
Excessive speed	Speed not excessive
Evidence of alcohol or drugs	
Group action	
Pre-mediated	
Serious injury/damage	
Serious risk	
Previous convictions and failures to respond to previous sentences, if relevant	

> IS IT SO SERIOUS THAT ONLY CUSTODY IS APPROPRIATE?
> IS IT SO SERIOUS ENOUGH FOR A COMMUNITY PENALTY?
> IS IT COMPENSATION, DISCHARGE OR FINE APPROPRIATE?

CONSIDER OFFENDER MITIGATION

eg.
Guilty plea: *for a timely guilty plea allow a discount of about a third*
Age, health (physical or mental)
Co-operation with the police
Voluntary compensation
Remorse

DECIDE YOUR SENTENCE

Compare your decision with the entry point - CUSTODY - and check your reasons if you have reached a different sentence

Endorse licence (3-11 points)

Disqualify at least 12 months unless special reasons apply

NB. COMPENSATION - Give reasons if not awarding compensation
NB. FINES - If imposing a fine, remember to increase or decrease the amount according to the financial circumstances of the offender

Police Act 1964 s.51
Triable only summarily
Penalty: Level 5 and/or 6 months

Assault on a Police Officer

ENTRY POINT / CUSTODY

(−)

CONSIDER THE SERIOUSNESS OF THE OFFENCE

eg.
Offence committed on bail
Any injuries caused
Gross disregard for police authority
Group action
Premeditated
Previous convictions and failures to respond
to previous sentences, if relevant

eg.
Impulsive action
Unaware that person was a Police Officer

(+)

IS IT SO SERIOUS THAT ONLY CUSTODY IS APPROPRIATE?
IS IT SERIOUS ENOUGH FOR A COMMUNITY PENALTY?
IS COMPENSATION, DISCHARGE OR FINE APPROPRIATE?

CONSIDER OFFENDER MITIGATION

eg.
Guilty plea: *for a timely guilty plea allow a discount of about a third*
Age, health (physical or mental)
Co-operation with the police
Voluntary compensation
Remorse

DECIDE YOUR SENTENCE

Compare your decision with the entry point - CUSTODY - and check your reasons if you have
reached a different sentence

NB. COMPENSATION - Give reasons if not awarding compensation
NB. FINES - If imposing a fine, remember to increase or decrease the amount according to the
financial circumstances of the offender

Theft Act 1968 s.9
Triable either way - see Mode of Trial Guidelines
Penalty: Level 5 and/or 6 months

Burglary (Dwelling)

ENTRY POINT / CUSTODY

(−)

CONSIDER THE SERIOUSNESS OF THE OFFENCE

eg.
Offence committed on bail
Deliberately frightening occupants
Group offence
Night time
Professional operation
Soiling, ransacking, damage
Previous convictions and failures to respond
to previous sentences, if relevant

eg.
Day time
Low value
No damage or disturbance
No forcible entry

(+)

IS IT SO SERIOUS THAT ONLY CUSTODY IS APPROPRIATE?
IS IT SERIOUS ENOUGH FOR A COMMUNITY PENALTY?
IS COMPENSATION, DISCHARGE OR FINE APPROPRIATE?

CONSIDER OFFENDER MITIGATION

eg.
Guilty plea: *for a timely guilty plea allow a discount of about a third*
Age, health (physical or mental)
Co-operation with the police
Voluntary compensation
Remorse

DECIDE YOUR SENTENCE

Compare your decision with the entry point - CUSTODY - and check your reasons if you have
reached a different sentence

NB. COMPENSATION - Give reasons if not awarding compensation
NB. FINES - If imposing a fine, remember to increase or decrease the amount according to the
financial circumstances of the offender

Common Assault

As charge sheet
Triable only summary
Penalty: Level 5 and/or 6 months

ENTRY POINT ⟋ **COMMUNITY PENALTY**

(+) ⊕ **CONSIDER THE SERIOUSNESS OF THE OFFENCE** (−) ⊖

eg.
- Offence committed on bail
- Group action
- Offender in position of authority
- Premediated
- Victim particularly vulnerable
- Victim public servant
- Previous convictions and failures to respond to previous sentences, if relevant

eg.
- Impulsive action
- Provocation
- Trivial nature of action

IS IT SERIOUS ENOUGH FOR A COMMUNITY PENALTY?
IS COMPENSATION, DISCHARGE OR FINE APPROPRIATE, OR
IS IT SO SERIOUS THAT ONLY CUSTODY IS APPROPRIATE?

CONSIDER OFFENDER MITIGATION

eg.
- Guilty plea: *for a timely guilty plea allow a discount of about a third*
- Age, health (physical or mental)
- Co-operation with the police
- Voluntary compensation
- Remorse

DECIDE YOUR SENTENCE

Compare your decision with the entry point - COMMUNITY PENALTY - and check your reasons if you have reached a different sentence

NB. COMPENSATION - Give reasons if not awarding compensation
NB. FINES - If imposing a fine, remember to increase or decrease the amount according to the financial circumstances of the offender

---

Burglary (Non-dwelling)

Theft Act 1968 s.9
Triable either way - see Mode of Trial Guidelines
Penalty: Level 5 and/or 6 months

ENTRY POINT ⟋ **COMMUNITY PENALTY**

(+) ⊕ **CONSIDER THE SERIOUSNESS OF THE OFFENCE** (−) ⊖

eg.
- Offence committed on bail
- Deliberately frightening occupants
- Group offence
- Night time
- Professional operation
- Ram raiding
- Soiling, ransacking, damage
- Previous convictions and failures to respond to previous sentences, if relevant

eg.
- Day time
- Low value
- No damage or disturbance
- No forcible entry

IS IT SERIOUS ENOUGH FOR A COMMUNITY PENALTY?
IS COMPENSATION, DISCHARGE OR FINE APPROPRIATE, OR
IS IT SO SERIOUS THAT ONLY CUSTODY IS APPROPRIATE?

CONSIDER OFFENDER MITIGATION

eg.
- Guilty plea: *for a timely guilty plea allow a discount of about a third*
- Age, health (physical or mental)
- Co-operation with the police
- Voluntary compensation
- Remorse

DECIDE YOUR SENTENCE

Compare your decision with the entry point - COMMUNITY PENALTY - and check your reasons if you have reached a different sentence

NB. COMPENSATION - Give reasons if not awarding compensation
NB. FINES - If imposing a fine, remember to increase or decrease the amount according to the financial circumstances of the offender

Careless Driving

Road Traffic Act 1988 s.3
Triable only summarily
Penalty: Level 4
Must endorse: (3-9 points)
May disqualify

ENTRY POINT / **FINE**

CONSIDER THE SERIOUSNESS OF THE OFFENCE

eg.
- Excessive speed
- High degree of carelessness
- Serious risk
- Offence committed on bail
- Previous convictions and failures to respond to previous sentences, if relevant

eg.
- Difficult weather conditions
- Minor risk
- Momentary lapse
- Negligible/parking damage

IS COMPENSATION, DISCHARGE OR FINE APPROPRIATE?
IS IT SERIOUS ENOUGH FOR A COMMUNITY PENALTY?
(PROBATION IS THE ONLY AVAILABLE COMMUNITY PENALTY FOR THIS OFFENCE)

CONSIDER OFFENDER MITIGATION

eg.
- Guilty plea: *for a timely guilty plea allow a discount of about a third*
- Co-operation with the police
- Voluntary compensation
- Remorse

DECIDE YOUR SENTENCE

Remember injury or damage cannot be *equated* with the degree of carelessness but may *indicate* it

Compare your decision with the entry point - FINE - and check your reasons if you have reached a different sentence

Guideline fine for this offence is £180 which reflects the average seriousness of an offence of this type

Endorse licence (3-9 points) and, if more serious, consider other measures (including disqualification until test passed if appropriate)

NB. FINES - If imposing a fine, remember to increase or decrease the amount according to the financial circumstances of the offender

---

Criminal Damage

Criminal Damage Act 1971 s.1
Triable either way or summarily only. Consult Clerk
Penalty: Either way - Level 5 and/or 6 months
Summarily - Level 4 and/or 3 months

ENTRY POINT / **FINE**

CONSIDER THE SERIOUSNESS OF THE OFFENCE

eg.
- Offence committed on bail
- Deliberate
- Fire raising
- Group offence
- Serious damage
- Previous convictions and failures to respond to previous sentences, it relevant

eg.
- Impulsive action
- Minor damage
- Provocation

IS COMPENSATION, DISCHARGE OR FINE APPROPRIATE?
IS IT SERIOUS ENOUGH FOR A COMMUNITY PENALTY?
IS IT SO SERIOUS THAT ONLY CUSTODY IS APPROPRIATE?

CONSIDER OFFENDER MITIGATION

eg.
- Guilty plea: *for a timely guilty plea allow a discount of about a third*
- Age, health (physical or mental)
- Co-operation with the police
- Voluntary compensation
- Remorse

DECIDE YOUR SENTENCE

Compare your decision with the entry point - FINE - and check your reasons if you have reached a different sentence

Guideline fine for this offence is £270 which reflects the average seriousness of an offence of this type

NB. COMPENSATION - Give reasons if not awarding compensation
NB. FINES - If imposing a fine, remember to increase or decrease the amount according to the financial circumstances of the offender

Driving — no insurance

Road Traffic Act 1988 s.143
Triable only summarily
Penalty: Level 5
Must endorse: (6-8 points)
May disqualify

ENTRY POINT / FINE

(+) CONSIDER THE SERIOUSNESS OF THE OFFENCE (−)

eg.
- Deliberate driving without insurance
- LGV, HGV, PCV, PSV or minicabs
- No reference to insurance ever having been held
- Offence committed on bail
- Previous convictions and failures to respond to previous sentences, if relevant

eg.
- Accidental oversight
- Genuine mistake
- Insurance held but clearly not covering the driver or use
- Recently expired insurance
  — weeks?
  — months?
- Responsibility for providing insurance resting with another - the parent/owner/lender/hirer.
- Smaller vehicle, eg. moped

> *IS COMPENSATION, DISCHARGE OR FINE APPROPRIATE?*
> *IS IT SERIOUS ENOUGH FOR A COMMUNITY PENALTY FOR THIS OFFENCE?*
> *(PROBATION IS THE ONLY AVAILABLE COMMUNITY PENALTY FOR THIS OFFENCE)*

CONSIDER OFFENDER MITIGATION

eg.
- Guilty plea: *for a timely guilty plea allow a discount of about a third*
- Co-operation with the police
- Remorse

DECIDE YOUR SENTENCE

Compare your decision with the entry point - FINE - and check your reasons if you have reached a different sentence

Guideline fine for this offence is £540 (and £660 for LGV/PCV) which reflects the average seriousness of an offence of this type. The court should have regard to the amount of the insurance premium.

Endorse licence (6-8 points)

IF DELIBERATE THE COURT SHOULD DISQUALIFY

NB. FINES - If imposing a fine, remember to increase or decrease the amount according to the financial circumstances of the offender

---

Dangerous Driving

Road Traffic Act 1988 s.2
Triable either way - see Mode of Trial Guidelines
Penalty: Level 5 and/or 6 months
Must endorse and disqualify at least 12 months
Must endorse (3-11 points) if not disqualified

ENTRY POINT / COMMUNITY PENALTY

(+) CONSIDER THE SERIOUSNESS OF THE OFFENCE (−)

eg.
- Offence committed on bail
- Avoiding detection or apprehension
- Competitive driving, racing, showing off
- Disregard of warnings eg. from passengers or others in vicinity
- Evidence of alcohol or drugs
- Excessive speed
- Prolonged, persistent, deliberate bad driving
- Serious risk
- Previous convictions and failures to respond to previous sentences, if relevant

eg.
- Momentary risk not fully appreciated
- No alcohol or drugs involved
- Single incident
- Speed not excessive

> *IS IT SERIOUS ENOUGH FOR A COMMUNITY PENALTY?*
> *IS COMPENSATION, DISCHARGE OR FINE APPROPRIATE, OR*
> *IS IT SO SERIOUS THAT ONLY CUSTODY IS APPROPRIATE?*

CONSIDER OFFENDER MITIGATION

eg.
- Guilty plea: *for a timely guilty plea allow a discount of about a third*
- Age, health (physical or mental)
- Co-operation with the police
- Voluntary compensation
- Remorse

DECIDE YOUR SENTENCE

Remember injury or damage cannot be *equated* with the degree of danger but may *indicate* it

Compare your decision with the entry point - COMMUNITY PENALTY - and check your reasons if you have reached a different sentence

Endorse licence (3-11 points) and disqualify at least 12 months unless special reasons apply

Order re-test

NB. FINES - If imposing a fine, remember to increase or decrease the amount according to the financial circumstances of the offender

Class A Drugs —
production, supply, possession
with intent to supply

Misuse of Drugs Act 1971
Triable either way - see Mode of Trial Guidelines
Penalty: Level 5 and/or 6 months

COMMIT FOR TRIAL

These offences are not usually dealt with in Magistrates' Courts and should normally be committed to the Crown Court for trial

---

Driving while disqualified
by Court Order

Road Traffic Act 1988 s.103
Triable only summarily
Penalty: Level 5 and/or 6 months
Must endorse: 6 points: may disqualify

ENTRY POINT /

CUSTODY

(+) CONSIDER THE SERIOUSNESS OF THE OFFENCE (-)

eg.
Offence committed on bail
Efforts to avoid detection
Long distance drive
Planned, long term evasion
Recent disqualification
Previous convictions and failures to respond
to previous sentences, if relevant

eg.
Emergency established
Short distance driven

IS IT SO SERIOUS THAT ONLY CUSTODY IS APPROPRIATE?
IS IT SERIOUS ENOUGH FOR A COMMUNITY PENALTY?
IS COMPENSATION, DISCHARGE OR FINE APPROPRIATE?

CONSIDER OFFENDER MITIGATION

eg.
Guilty plea: *for a timely guilty plea allow a discount of about a third*
Age, health (physical or mental)
Co-operation with the police
Remorse

DECIDE YOUR SENTENCE

Compare your decision with the entry point - CUSTODY - and check your reasons if you have reached a different sentence

Endorse licence (6 points) and consider disqualification

NB. FINES - If imposing a fine, remember to increase or decrease the amount according to the financial circumstances of the offender

Class B Drugs — Supply

Possession with intent to supply

Misuse of Drugs Act 1971
Triable either way - see Mode of Trial Guidelines
Penalty: Level 5 and/or 6 months

ENTRY POINT ➤ **COMMIT FOR TRIAL UNLESS SMALL SCALE SUPPLY, OTHERWISE CUSTODY**

(−) CONSIDER THE SERIOUSNESS OF THE OFFENCE (+)

eg. Small amount

Offence committed on bail
Commercial production
Large amount
Previous convictions and failures to respond to previous sentences, if relevant

IS IT SO SERIOUS THAT ONLY CUSTODY IS APPROPRIATE?
IS IT SERIOUS ENOUGH FOR A COMMUNITY PENALTY?
IS COMPENSATION, DISCHARGE OR FINE APPROPRIATE?

CONSIDER OFFENDER MITIGATION

eg. Guilty plea: for a timely guilty plea allow a discount of about a third
Age, health (physical or mental)
Co-operation with the police
Remorse

DECIDE YOUR SENTENCE

Compare your decision with the entry point - CUSTODY - and check your reasons if you have reached a different sentence

Consider forfeiture of all drugs and equipment

NB. FINES - If imposing a fine, remember to increase or decrease the amount according to the financial circumstances of the offender

---

Class A Drugs — Possession

Misuse of Drugs Act 1971
Triable either way - see Mode of Trial Guidelines
Penalty: Level 5 and/or 6 months

ENTRY POINT ➤ **COMMUNITY PENALTY**

(−) CONSIDER THE SERIOUSNESS OF THE OFFENCE (+)

eg. Very small quantity

Offence committed on bail
An amount other than a very small quantity
Previous convictions and failures to respond to previous sentences, if relevant

IS IT SERIOUS ENOUGH FOR A COMMUNITY PENALTY?
IS COMPENSATION, DISCHARGE OR FINE APPROPRIATE, OR
IS IT SO SERIOUS THAT ONLY CUSTODY IS APPROPRIATE?

CONSIDER OFFENDER MITIGATION

eg. Guilty plea: for a timely guilty plea allow a discount of about a third
Age, health (physical or mental)
Co-operation with the police
Remorse

DECIDE YOUR SENTENCE

Compare your decision with the entry point - COMMUNITY PENALTY - and check your reasons if you have reached a different sentence

Consider forfeiture of all drugs and equipment

NB. FINES - If imposing a fine, remember to increase or decrease the amount according to the financial circumstances of the offender

Class B Drugs — Possession

Misuse of Drugs Acts 1971
Triable either way - see Mode of Trial Guidelines
Penalty: £500 and/or 3 months

ENTRY POINT / FINE

(+) CONSIDER THE SERIOUSNESS OF THE OFFENCE (−)

eg.
Offence committed on bail
Large amount
Previous convictions and failures to respond
to previous sentences, if relevant

eg. Small amount

IS COMPENSATION, DISCHARGE OR FINE APPROPRIATE?
IS IT SERIOUS ENOUGH FOR A COMMUNITY PENALTY?
IS IT SO SERIOUS THAT ONLY CUSTODY IS APPROPRIATE?

CONSIDER OFFENDER MITIGATION

eg.
Guilty plea: for a timely guilty plea allow a discount of about a third
Age, health (physical or mental)
Co-operation with the police
Remorse

DECIDE YOUR SENTENCE

Compare your decision with the entry point - FINE - and check your reasons if you have
reached a different sentence

Guideline fine for this offence is £180 which reflects the average seriousness of an offence of
this type

Consider forfeiture of all drugs and equipment

NB. FINES - If imposing a fine, remember to increase or decrease the amount according to the
financial circumstances of the offender

Cultivation of Cannabis

Misuse of Drugs Act 1971
Triable either way - see Mode of Trial Guidelines
Penalty: Level 5 and/or 6 months

ENTRY POINT / FINE

(+) CONSIDER THE SERIOUSNESS OF THE OFFENCE (−)

eg.
Offence committed on bail
Commercial cultivation
Large quantity
Previous convictions and failures to respond
to previous sentences, if relevant

eg. Small scale cultivation for personal use

IS COMPENSATION, DISCHARGE OR FINE APPROPRIATE?
IS IT SERIOUS ENOUGH FOR A COMMUNITY PENALTY?
IS IT SO SERIOUS THAT ONLY CUSTODY IS APPROPRIATE?

CONSIDER OFFENDER MITIGATION

eg.
Guilty plea: for a timely guilty plea allow a discount of about a third
Age, health (physical or mental)
Co-operation with the police
Remorse

DECIDE YOUR SENTENCE

Compare your decision with the entry point - FINE - and check your reasons if you have
reached a different sentence

Guideline fine for this offence is £180 which reflects the average seriousness of an offence of
this type

Consider forfeiture of all drugs and equipment

NB. FINES - If imposing a fine, remember to increase or decrease the amount according to the
financial circumstances of the offender

Failing to Stop / Failing to Report

Road Traffic Act 1988 s. 170 (as amended)
Triable only summarily
Penalty: Level 5 and/or 6 months
Must endorse: 5-10 points: may disqualify

ENTRY POINT — **FINE**

(−) CONSIDER THE SERIOUSNESS OF THE OFFENCE

eg.
- Offence committed on bail
- Evidence of drinking
- Serious injury and failure to to stop or remain at scene
- Serious injury and/or serious damage
- Previous convictions and failures to respond to previous sentences, if relevant

eg.
- Failed to stop but reported
- Negligible damage
- No one at scene but failed to report
- Stayed at scene but failed to give full particulars
- Stayed at scene but left before giving full particulars

IS COMPENSATION, DISCHARGE OR FINE APPROPRIATE?
IS IT SERIOUS ENOUGH FOR A COMMUNITY PENALTY?
IS IT SO SERIOUS THAT ONLY CUSTODY IS APPROPRIATE?

(+) CONSIDER OFFENDER MITIGATION

eg.
- Guilty plea: *for a timely guilty plea allow a discount of about a third*
- Age, health (physical or mental)
- Co-operation with the police
- Voluntary compensation
- Remorse

DECIDE YOUR SENTENCE

Compare your decision with the entry point - FINE - and check your reasons if you have reached a different sentence

Guideline fine for this offence is £360 which reflects the average seriousness of an offence of this type

Endorse licence (5-10 points) and consider disqualification

NB. COMPENSATION - Give reasons if not awarding compensation
NB. FINES - If imposing a fine, remember to increase or decrease the amount according to the financial circumstances of the offender

---

Drunk and Disorderly

Criminal Justice Act 1967 s.91
Triable only summarily
Penalty: Level 3

ENTRY POINT — **FINE**

(−) CONSIDER THE SERIOUSNESS OF THE OFFENCE

eg.
- Offence committed on bail
- Busy public place
- Offensive language or behaviour
- With group
- Previous convictions and failures to respond to previous sentences, if relevant

eg.
- Account should be taken of any time spent in custody

IS COMPENSATION, DISCHARGE OR FINE APPROPRIATE?
IS IT SERIOUS ENOUGH FOR A COMMUNITY PENALTY?
(PROBATION IS THE ONLY AVAILABLE COMMUNITY PENALTY FOR THIS OFFENCE)

(+) CONSIDER OFFENDER MITIGATION

eg.
- Guilty plea: *for a timely guilty plea allow a discount of about a third*
- Age, health (physical or mental)
- Co-operation with the police
- Remorse

DECIDE YOUR SENTENCE

Compare your decision with the entry point - FINE - and check your reasons if you have reached a different sentence

Guideline fine for this offence is £90 which reflects the average seriousness of an offence of this type

NB. COMPENSATION - Give reasons if not awarding compensation
NB. FINES - If imposing a fine, remember to increase or decrease the amount according to the financial circumstances of the offender

Fear or provocation of Violence

Public Order Act 1986 s.4
Triable only summarily
Penalty: Level 5 and/or 6 months

ENTRY POINT / COMMUNITY PENALTY

+ CONSIDER THE SERIOUSNESS OF THE OFFENCE −

eg.
Offence committed on bail
Busy public place
Group action
People put in fear
Vulnerable victims
Previous convictions and failures to respond
to previous sentences, if relevant

eg.
Single offender

IS IT SERIOUS ENOUGH FOR A COMMUNITY PENALTY?
IS COMPENSATION, DISCHARGE OR FINE APPROPRIATE, OR
IS IT SO SERIOUS THAT ONLY CUSTODY IS APPROPRIATE?

CONSIDER OFFENDER MITIGATION

eg.
Guilty plea: *for a timely guilty plea allow a discount of about a third*
Age, health (physical or mental)
Co-operation with the police
Voluntary compensation
Remorse

DECIDE YOUR SENTENCE

Compare your decision with the entry point - COMMUNITY PENALTY - and check your
reasons if you have reached a different sentence

NB. COMPENSATION - Give reasons if not awarding compensation
NB. FINES - If imposing a fine, remember to increase or decrease the amount according to the
financial circumstances of the offender

Handling Stolen Goods

Theft Act 1968 s.22
Triable either way - see Mode of Trial Guidelines
Penalty: Level 5 and/or 6 months

ENTRY POINT / COMMUNITY PENALTY

+ CONSIDER THE SERIOUSNESS OF THE OFFENCE −

eg.
Offence committed on bail
Adult involving children
High value
Organiser or distributor
Stolen to order
Previous convictions and failures to respond
to previous sentences, if relevant

eg.
Impulsive action
Low value
Single item for personal use

IS IT SERIOUS ENOUGH FOR A COMMUNITY PENALTY?
IS COMPENSATION, DISCHARGE OR FINE APPROPRIATE, OR
IS IT SO SERIOUS THAT ONLY CUSTODY IS APPROPRIATE?

CONSIDER OFFENDER MITIGATION

eg.
Guilty plea: *for a timely guilty plea allow a discount of about a third*
Age, health (physical or mental)
Co-operation with the police
Voluntary compensation
Remorse

DECIDE YOUR SENTENCE

Compare your decision with the entry point - COMMUNITY PENALTY - and check your
reasons if you have reached a different sentence

NB. COMPENSATION - Give reasons if not awarding compensation
NB. FINES - If imposing a fine, remember to increase or decrease the amount according to the
financial circumstances of the offender

Making Off without Payment

Theft Act 1978 s.3
Triable either way - see Mode of Trial Guidelines
Penalty: Level 5 and/or 6 months

ENTRY POINT ► **FINE**

CONSIDER THE SERIOUSNESS OF THE OFFENCE

(+) eg.:
Offence committed on bail
Deliberate plan
Large sum
Two or more involved
Victim particularly vulnerable
Previous convictions and failures to respond to previous sentences, if relevant

(–) eg.:
Impulsive action

IS COMPENSATION, DISCHARGE OR FINE APPROPRIATE?
IS IT SERIOUS ENOUGH FOR A COMMUNITY PENALTY?
IS IT SO SERIOUS THAT ONLY CUSTODY IS APPROPRIATE?

CONSIDER OFFENDER MITIGATION

eg.:
Guilty plea: *for a timely guilty plea allow a discount of about a third*
Age, health (physical or mental)
Co-operation with the police
Voluntary compensation
Remorse

DECIDE YOUR SENTENCE

Compare your decision with the entry point - FINE - and check your reasons if you have reached a different sentence

Guideline fine for this offence is £180 which reflects the average seriousness of an offence of this type

NB. COMPENSATION - Give reasons if not awarding compensation
NB. FINES - If imposing a fine, remember to increase or decrease the amount according to the financial circumstances of the offender

---

Harassment, Alarm or Distress

Public Order Act 1986 s.5
Triable only summary
Penalty: Level 3

ENTRY POINT ► **FINE**

CONSIDER THE SERIOUSNESS OF THE OFFENCE

(+) eg.:
Offence committed on bail
Group action
Vulnerable victim
Previous convictions and failures to respond to previous sentences, if relevant

(–) eg.:
Single offender

IS COMPENSATION, DISCHARGE OR FINE APPROPRIATE?
IS IT SERIOUS ENOUGH FOR A COMMUNITY PENALTY?
(PROBATION IS THE ONLY AVAILABLE COMMUNITY PENALTY FOR THIS OFFENCE)

CONSIDER OFFENDER MITIGATION

eg.:
Guilty plea: *for a timely guilty plea allow a discount of about a third*
Age, health (physical or mental)
Co-operation with the police
Voluntary compensation
Remorse

DECIDE YOUR SENTENCE

Compare your decision with the entry point - FINE - and check your reasons if you have reached a different sentence

Guideline fine for this offence is £180 which reflects the average seriousness of an offence of this type

NB. COMPENSATION - Give reasons if not awarding compensation
NB. FINES - If imposing a fine, remember to increase or decrease the amount according to the financial circumstances of the offender

Police Act 1964 s.51
Triable only summarily
Penalty: Level 3 and/or 1 month

Obstructing a
Police Officer

ENTRY POINT ⟋ | FINE | ⊖

CONSIDER THE SERIOUSNESS OF THE OFFENCE ⊕

eg.
Offence committed on bail
Gross disregard for Police authority
Group action
Premeditated
Previous convictions and failures to respond
to previous sentences, if relevant

eg.
Genuine misjudgement
Impulsive action
Minor obstruction
Unaware that person was a Police Officer

IS IT COMPENSATION, DISCHARGE OR FINE APPROPRIATE?
IS IT SERIOUS ENOUGH FOR A COMMUNITY PENALTY?
IS IT SO SERIOUS THAT ONLY CUSTODY IS APPROPRIATE?

CONSIDER OFFENDER MITIGATION

eg.
Guilty plea: for a timely guilty plea allow a discount of about a third
Age, health (physical or mental)
Co-operation with the police
Voluntary compensation
Remorse

DECIDE YOUR SENTENCE

Compare your decision with the entry point - FINE - and check your reasons if you have reached a different sentence

Guideline fine for this offence is £180 which reflects the average seriousness of an offence of this type

NB. COMPENSATION - Give reasons if not awarding compensation
NB. FINES - If imposing a fine, remember to increase or decrease the amount according to the financial circumstances of the offender

---

Obtaining by
Deception

Theft Act 1968 s.15
Triable either way - see Mode of Trial Guidelines
Penalty: Level 5 and/or 6 months

ENTRY POINT ⟋ | COMMUNITY PENALTY | ⊖

CONSIDER THE SERIOUSNESS OF THE OFFENCE ⊕

eg.
Offence committed on bail
Committed over lengthy period
Large sums or valuable goods
Two or more involved
Victim particularly vulnerable
Previous convictions and failures to respond
to previous sentences, if relevant

eg.
Impulsive action
Short period
Small sum

IS IT SERIOUS ENOUGH FOR A COMMUNITY PENALTY?
IS IT COMPENSATION, DISCHARGE OR FINE APPROPRIATE, OR
IS IT SO SERIOUS THAT ONLY CUSTODY IS APPROPRIATE?

CONSIDER OFFENDER MITIGATION

eg.
Guilty plea: for a timely guilty plea allow a discount of about a third
Age, health (physical or mental)
Co-operation with the police
Compensation
Remorse

DECIDE YOUR SENTENCE

Compare your decision with the entry point - COMMUNITY PENALTY - and check your reasons if you have reached a different sentence

NB. COMPENSATION - Give reasons if not awarding compensation
NB. FINES - If imposing a fine, remember to increase or decrease the amount according to the financial circumstances of the offender

Social Security - false representation to obtain benefit

Social Security Act 1986 s.55
Triable only summarily
Penalty: Level 5 and/or 3 months

ENTRY POINT ✓ → **COMMUNITY PENALTY**

(+) CONSIDER THE SERIOUSNESS OF THE OFFENCE (−)

eg.	eg.
Offence committed on bail	Ignorance of regulations
Fraudulent claims over a long period	Offence of omission
Large amount	
Organised group offence	
Planned deception	
Previous convictions and failures to respond	
to previous sentences, if relevant	

IS IT SERIOUS ENOUGH FOR A COMMUNITY PENALTY?
IS COMPENSATION, DISCHARGE OR FINE APPROPRIATE, OR
IS IT SO SERIOUS THAT ONLY CUSTODY IS APPROPRIATE?

CONSIDER OFFENDER MITIGATION

eg.
Guilty plea: *for a timely guilty plea allow a discount of about a third*
Age, health (physical or mental)
Co-operation with the prosecuting authority
Voluntary compensation
Remorse

DECIDE YOUR SENTENCE

Compare your decision with the entry point - COMMUNITY PENALTY - and check your reasons if you have reached a different sentence

NB. COMPENSATION - Give reasons if not awarding compensation
NB. FINES - If imposing a fine, remember to increase or decrease the amount according to the financial circumstances of the offender

---

Taking Vehicle without Consent

Theft Act 1968 s.12
Triable only summarily
Penalty: Level 5 and/or 6 months
May disqualify

ENTRY POINT ✓ → **COMMUNITY PENALTY**

(+) CONSIDER THE SERIOUSNESS OF THE OFFENCE (−)

eg.	eg.
Offence committed on bail	Keys left in car
Group action	Misunderstanding with owner
Premeditated	
Related damage	
Vulnerable victim	
Previous convictions and failures to respond	
to previous sentences, if relevant	

IS IT SERIOUS ENOUGH FOR A COMMUNITY PENALTY?
IS COMPENSATION, DISCHARGE OR FINE APPROPRIATE, OR
IS IT SO SERIOUS THAT ONLY CUSTODY IS APPROPRIATE?

CONSIDER OFFENDER MITIGATION

eg.
Guilty plea: *for a timely guilty plea allow a discount of about a third*
Age, health (physical or mental)
Co-operation with the police
Voluntary compensation
Remorse

DECIDE YOUR SENTENCE

Compare your decision with the entry point - COMMUNITY PENALTY - and check your reasons if you have reached a different sentence

Consider disqualification

NB. COMPENSATION - Give reasons if not awarding compensation
NB. FINES - If imposing a fine, remember to increase or decrease the amount according to the financial circumstances of the offender

Theft (General)

Theft Act 1968 s.1
Triable either way - see Mode of Trial Guidelines
Penalty: Level 5 and/or 6 months

ENTRY POINT ✔   **FINE**

CONSIDER THE SERIOUSNESS OF THE OFFENCE

(+)

eg.
- Offence committed on bail
- Large Amount
- Planned
- Sophisticated
- Vulnerable victim
- Previous convictions and failures to respond to previous sentences, if relevant

eg.
- Impulsive action
- Small amount
- Voluntary restitution

(−)

IS COMPENSATION, DISCHARGE OR FINE APPROPRIATE?
IS IT SERIOUS ENOUGH FOR A COMMUNITY PENALTY?
IS IT SO SERIOUS THAT ONLY CUSTODY IS APPROPRIATE?

CONSIDER OFFENDER MITIGATION

eg.
- Guilty plea: for a timely guilty plea allow a discount of about a third
- Age, health (physical or mental)
- Co-operation with the police
- Voluntary compensation
- Remorse

DECIDE YOUR SENTENCE

Compare your decision with the entry point - FINE - and check your reasons if you have reached a different sentence

Guideline fine for this offence is £270 which reflects the average seriousness of an offence of this type

NB. COMPENSATION - Give reasons if not awarding compensation
NB. FINES - If imposing a fine, remember to increase or decrease the amount according to the financial circumstances of the offender

---

Theft from a Shop

Theft Act 1968 s.1
Triable either way - see Mode of Trial Guidelines
Penalty: Level 5 and/or 6 months

ENTRY POINT ✔   **FINE**

CONSIDER THE SERIOUSNESS OF THE OFFENCE

(+)

eg.
- Offence committed on bail
- Adult involving children
- High value
- Organised teams
- Planned
- Previous convictions and failures to respond to previous sentences, if relevant

eg.
- Impulsive action
- Low value

(−)

IS COMPENSATION, DISCHARGE OR FINE APPROPRIATE?
IS IT SERIOUS ENOUGH FOR A COMMUNITY PENALTY?
IS IT SO SERIOUS THAT ONLY CUSTODY IS APPROPRIATE?

CONSIDER OFFENDER MITIGATION

eg.
- Guilty plea: for a timely guilty plea allow a discount of about a third
- Age, health (physical or mental)
- Co-operation with the police
- Voluntary compensation
- Remorse

DECIDE YOUR SENTENCE

Compare your decision with the entry point - FINE - and check your reasons if you have reached a different sentence

Guideline fine for this offence is £270 which reflects the average seriousness of an offence of this type

NB. COMPENSATION - Give reasons if not awarding compensation
NB. FINES - If imposing a fine, remember to increase or decrease the amount according to the financial circumstances of the offender

Theft Act 1968 s.1
Triable either way - see Mode of Trial Guidelines
Penalty: Level 5 and/or 6 months

Theft from Vehicle

ENTRY POINT	COMMUNITY PENALTY

CONSIDER THE SERIOUSNESS OF THE OFFENCE (−)

(+)

eg.
- Offence committed on bail
- High value
- Organised team
- Planned
- Related damage
- Previous convictions and failures to respond to previous sentences, if relevant

eg.
- Car unlocked
- Impulsive action

IS IT SERIOUS ENOUGH FOR A COMMUNITY PENALTY?
IS COMPENSATION, DISCHARGE OR FINE APPROPRIATE, OR
IS IT SO SERIOUS THAT ONLY CUSTODY IS APPROPRIATE?

CONSIDER OFFENDER MITIGATION

eg.
- Guilty plea: *for a timely guilty plea allow a discount of about a third*
- Age, health (physical or mental)
- Co-operation with the police
- Voluntary compensation
- Remorse

DECIDE YOUR SENTENCE

Compare your decision with the entry point - COMMUNITY PENALTY - and check your reasons if you have reached a different sentence

NB. COMPENSATION - Give reasons if not awarding compensation
NB. FINES - If imposing a fine, remember to increase or decrease the amount according to the financial circumstances of the offender

---

Theft Act 1968 s.1
Triable either way - see Mode of Trial Guidelines
Penalty: Level 5 and/or 6 months

Theft in Breach of Trust

ENTRY POINT	COMMUNITY PENALTY

CONSIDER THE SERIOUSNESS OF THE OFFENCE (−)

eg.
- Offence committed on bail
- Casting suspicion on others
- Committed over a period
- Large amount
- Planned
- Senior employee
- Sophisticated
- Vulnerable victim
- Previous convictions and failures to respond to previous sentences, if relevant

eg.
- Impulsive action
- Newly employed junior
- Single item
- Small amount

IS IT SERIOUS ENOUGH FOR A COMMUNITY PENALTY?
IS COMPENSATION, DISCHARGE OR FINE APPROPRIATE, OR
IS IT SO SERIOUS THAT ONLY CUSTODY IS APPROPRIATE?

CONSIDER OFFENDER MITIGATION

eg.
- Guilty plea: *for a timely guilty plea allow a discount of about a third*
- Age, health (physical or mental)
- Co-operation with the police
- Voluntary compensation
- Remorse

DECIDE YOUR SENTENCE

Compare your decision with the entry point - COMMUNITY PENALTY - and check your reasons if you have reached a different sentence

NB. COMPENSATION - Give reasons if not awarding compensation
NB. FINES - If imposing a fine, remember to increase or decrease the amount according to the financial circumstances of the offender

Violent Disorder

Public Order Act 1986 s.2
Triable either way - see Mode of Trial Guidelines
Penalty: Level 5 and/or 6 months

ENTRY POINT /	CUSTODY

 CONSIDER THE SERIOUSNESS OF THE OFFENCE

eg.
- Offence committed on bail
- Busy public place
- Large group
- People put in fear
- Vulnerable victims
- Previous convictions and failures to respond to previous sentences, if relevant

> *IS IT SO SERIOUS THAT ONLY CUSTODY IS APPROPRIATE?*
> *IS IT SERIOUS ENOUGH FOR A COMMUNITY PENALTY?*
> *IS COMPENSATION, DISCHARGE OR FINE APPROPRIATE?*

CONSIDER OFFENDER MITIGATION

eg.
- Guilty plea: for a timely guilty plea allow a discount of about a third
- Age, health (physical or mental)
- Co-operation with the police
- Voluntary compensation
- Remorse

DECIDE YOUR SENTENCE

Compare your decision with the entry point - CUSTODY - and check your reasons if you have reached a different sentence

NB. COMPENSATION - Give reasons if not awarding compensation

NB. FINES - If imposing a fine, remember to increase or decrease the amount according to the financial circumstances of the offender

---

TV Licence Evasion

Wireless Telegraphy Act 1949 s.1
Triable only summarily
Penalty: Level 3

ENTRY POINT /	FINE

 CONSIDER THE SERIOUSNESS OF THE OFFENCE

eg.
- Offence committed on bail
- Deliberate evasion
- Lengthy unlicensed use
- Previous convictions and failures to respond to previous sentences, if relevant

eg.
- Accidental oversight
- Confusion of responsibility
- Very short unlicensed use

> *IS COMPENSATION, DISCHARGE OR FINE APPROPRIATE?*
> *IS IT SERIOUS ENOUGH FOR A COMMUNITY PENALTY?*
> *(PROBATION IS THE ONLY AVAILABLE COMMUNITY PENALTY FOR THIS OFFENCE)*

CONSIDER OFFENDER MITIGATION

eg.
- Guilty plea: for a timely guilty plea allow a discount of about a third
- Age, health (physical or mental)
- Co-operation with the prosecuting authority
- Remorse/prompt renewal of licence
- Visitor to the premises

DECIDE YOUR SENTENCE

Compare your decision with the entry point - FINE - and check your reasons if you have reached a different sentence

Guideline fines for this offence are £180 (Colour) £90 (Mono) which reflect the average seriousness of an offence of this type

NB. FINES - If imposing a fine, remember to increase or decrease the amount according to the financial circumstances of the offender

Offences Against the Person Act 1861 s.20
Triable either way - see Mode of Trial Guidelines
Penalty: Level 5 and/or 6 months

Wounding — Grievous Bodily Harm

ENTRY POINT ⋗

CUSTODY

– +

CONSIDER THE SERIOUSNESS OF THE OFFENCE

eg.
Offence committed on bail
Deliberate kicking
Extensive injuries
Group action
Offender in position of authority
Premeditated
Victim particularly vulnerable
Victim serving public
Weapon
Previous convictions and failures to respond
to previous sentences, if relevant

eg.
Impulsive action
Provocation

IS IT SO SERIOUS THAT ONLY CUSTODY IS APPROPRIATE?
IS IT SERIOUS ENOUGH FOR A COMMUNITY PENALTY?
IS COMPENSATION, DISCHARGE OR FINE APPROPRIATE?

CONSIDER OFFENDER MITIGATION

eg.
Guilty plea: *for a timely guilty plea allow a discount of about a third*
Age, health (physical or mental)
Co-operation with the police
Voluntary compensation
Remorse

DECIDE YOUR SENTENCE

Compare your decision with the entry point - CUSTODY - check your reasons if you have
reached a different sentence

NB. COMPENSATION - Give reasons if not awarding compensation
NB. FINES - If imposing a fine, remember to increase or decrease the amount according to the
financial circumstances of the offender

Suggestions for Road Traffic Offence Penalties

HOW TO USE THE 'SUGGESTIONS'

For the general approach, please refer to the main introduction, noting that it cannot be emphasised too strongly that THE LIST IS NOT A TARIFF.

The recommended approach for serious road-traffic offences is to use scales based on seriousness indicators. These suggestions offer a starting point based on an average offence without aggravating factors. However, please note that suggested starting points are now based on a NOT GUILTY plea to allow a DISCOUNT of up to a third to be given for a prompt guilty plea.

The seriousness of offences differs widely, especially in cases of careless driving, and many road traffic offences are more hazardous when speeds are higher. Experience has proved that drinking and driving offences account for very many accidents, injuries and deaths. The Court of Appeal has consistently upheld higher penalties for offenders with higher alcohol figures, and it is suggested that penalties and especially periods of disqualification should reflect this. When fixing the size of a fine where an order of disqualification is also made, it should be remembered that the impact of disqualification varies from offender to offender and disqualification will frequently itself entail a very heavy financial burden.

The level of penalties must not become out of proportion compared to the level of fines for common criminal offences such as thefts from shops and assaults.

Variable Penalty Points
Variable penalty points offences imply greater variations in sentence. The fine will give a result adjusted to the financial circumstances of the offender but the penalty points chosen should correspond to the seriousness of the offence.

The Multiple Offender
Where on one occasion an offender is convicted of a large number of offences it is suggested that the court should also take an overall view and initially decide upon the maximum total amount of the fines which it is appropriate to impose for all the offences, even though this total may prove to be considerably less than the figure which would result from adding together all the suggested penalties involved.

Companies
When fining companies the position will depend on the financial standing of the company.

T R P Rudin
SECRETARY

Twelfth Edition
September 1993

The Magistrates' Association
28 Fitzroy Square, London W1P 6DD

IMPORTANT
These suggestions may be reproduced for the use of benches provided the front page is included.

The Magistrates' Association · Page 45 · Issue September 1993

THIS IS NOT A TARIFF and these Suggestions are to be used only as a starting point
Allow a discount of about a third for a timely guilty plea

SUGGESTIONS FOR COURTS' ASSESSMENT OF PENALTIES FOR MAIN TRAFFIC OFFENCES

The maximum standard levels are at present:

Level 1 - £200
Level 2 - £500
Level 3 - £1,000
Level 4 - £2,500
Level 5 - £5,000

D — Must disqualify at least 12 months (unless special reasons) and endorse.
(if disqualifying for a lengthy period, or if driving skill suspect, consider disqualifying until test passed)
E — Must endorse (unless special reasons) and may disqualify.
MD — May disqualify - no power to endorse or assign penalty points
The maximum penalties for 'goods vehicles' also apply to 'vehicles adapted to carry more than eight passengers'. (See offences 7, 8, 9, 21 and 41, 42 and 43)
† — Fixed penalty offences
◆ — Refer to Guidelines

OFFENCE	PENALTY POINTS	MAXIMUM PENALTY	COMMENTS	FINE
ACCIDENT				
1.◆ Failing to stop	5-10	Level 5 E and/or six months prison	**Refer to Guidelines:** Should disqualify if serious	£360
2.◆ Failing to report to the police	5-10	Level 5 E and/or six months prison	**Refer to Guidelines:** Should disqualify if serious	£360
ALCOHOL Over 35µg breath: 80mg blood: 107mg urine				
3. Drunken driving or driving with excess alcohol	(3 - 11)	Level 5 D and/or six months prison	See Excess Alcohol chart on page 51	
4. Refusing evidential specimen (driving)	(3 - 11)	Level 5 D and/or six months prison	D 18 months	£720
5. In charge drunk or with excess alcohol or refusing evidential specimen	10	Level 4 E and/or three months prison		£360
6. Refusing roadside breath test	4	Level 3 E		£180
DEFECTS				
7.† Brakes	3	Level 4 E but for goods vehicles etc. Level 5 E	Consider degree of responsibility Driver LGV/HGV Owner LGV/HGV Driver	£120 £300 £210
8.† Steering	3	Level 4 E but for goods vehicles etc. Level 5 E	Consider degree of responsibility Driver LGV/HGV Owner LGV/HGV Driver	£120 £300 £210
9.† Tyres (NB. Suggested penalty refers to each tyre)	3	Level 4 E but for goods vehicles etc. Level 5 E	Consider degree of responsibility Driver LGV/HGV Owner LGV/HGV Driver	£120 £300 £210
DISQUALIFIED				
10.◆ By court order	6	Level 5 E and/or six months prison	**Refer to Guidelines:** Entry point for this offence is CUSTODY	
DOCUMENTS				
11. Failing to produce		Level 3		£60

The Magistrates' Association · Page 46 · Issue September 1993

OFFENCE	PENALTY POINTS	MAXIMUM PENALTY	COMMENTS	FINE
DOUBLE WHITE LINES				
12.† Failing to comply with system	3	Level 3E		£120
DRIVING				
13.◆ Dangerous	(3 - 11)	Level 5 D and/or six months prison	Refer to Guidelines: Entry point for this offence is COMMUNITY PENALTY. Disqualify for at least the compulsory twelve months and order retest	
14.◆ Careless or inconsiderate	3 - 9	Level 4 E	Refer to Guidelines: Always consider degree of carelessness	£180
HELMET				
15.† No safety helmet	-	Level 2		£50
INSURANCE				
16.◆ No insurance	6 - 8	Level 5 E	LGV/PCV or taxi-cabs	£540 £660

In fixing the fine regard should be had as to whether the offence was deliberate or inadvertent, whether the offender was misled or any other mitigating circumstances and whether the 'user' or 'permitter' was responsible for the amount of the insurance premium. IF DELIBERATE THE COURT SHOULD DISQUALIFY. In any event the court must have regard to the offence.

OFFENCE	PENALTY POINTS	MAXIMUM PENALTY	COMMENTS	FINE
LICENCE OFFENCES AND LEARNER DRIVERS				
17.† Driving not in accordance with a licence	3 - 6 where endorsable	Level 3 in some cases E		see below
eg				
† no licence where could not be covered	3 - 6	Level 3 E		£150
† no licence where could be covered	-	Level 3		£30
† under age	3 - 6	Level 3 E		£120
† unsupervised in car	3 - 6	Level 3 E	Consider disqualification	£120
† learner motor cyclist with passenger	3 - 6	Level 3 E	Consider disqualification	£90
† no "L" plates	3 - 6	Level 3 E		£60
18.† No excise licence	-	Level 3 or 5 times annual duty (whichever greater)	Actual duty loss plus penalty of approximately twice that amount or £120 whichever greater	
19. No operator's licence	-	Level 4		£450
LIGHTS				
20.† Driving without lights	-	Level 3		£90

OFFENCE	PENALTY POINTS	MAXIMUM PENALTY	COMMENTS	FINE
LOADS				
21.† Construction & Use: Condition/Load etc - danger of injury by:				
† condition of vehicle or of accessories or equipment	3	Level 4 E but for goods vehicles etc. Level 5 E	Ordinary vehicle-driver/owner but consider degree of responsibility / LGV/HGV Driver / LGV/HGV Owner	£180 £300 £600
† purpose of use	3	Level 4 E but for goods vehicles etc. Level 5 E	Ordinary vehicle-driver/owner but consider degree of responsibility / LGV/HGV Driver / LGV/HGV Owner	£180 £300 £600
† number or manner of carriage of passengers	3	Level 4 E but for goods vehicles etc. Level 5 E	Ordinary vehicle-owner but consider degree of responsibility / LGV/HGV Driver / LGV/HGV Owner	£180 £300 £600
† weight, position or distribution of load	3	Level 4 E but for goods vehicles etc. Level 5 E	Ordinary vehicle-owner but consider degree of responsibility / LGV/HGV Driver / LGV/HGV Owner	£180 £300 £600
† insecure load	3	Level 4 but for goods vehicles etc. Level 5 E	Non-LGV/HGV Owner/Driver but consider degree of responsibility / Non-LGV/HGV Commercial / LGV/HGV Driver / LGV/HGV Owner	£150 £180 £360 £750
† overloading or exceeding maximum axle weight - commercial vehicle	-	Level 5	Non-LGV/HGV Driver but consider degree of responsibility / Non-LGV/HGV Owner / LGV/HGV Driver / LGV/HGV Owner	£180 £360 £360 £750

Suggestion refers to conviction on each charge. In addition, for overloading add £30 for each 1% of overload (ignoring the first 10%) but always have regard to commercial gain and damage to roads.

OFFENCE	PENALTY POINTS	MAXIMUM PENALTY	COMMENTS	FINE
OWNERSHIP/DRIVER				
22. Not supplying details of driver	3	Level 3 E		£210
Not notifying DVLA etc.	-	Level 3		£150
PARKING				
23.† Dangerous position	3	Level 3 E		£90
24.† On zig-zags by pedestrian crossing	3	Level 3 E		£90
25.† Obstruction	-	Level 3		£60
26.† Stopping on Clearway	-	Level 3		£60
PEDESTRIAN OR SCHOOL CROSSING				
27.† Offences other than parking (certain offences only)	3	Level 3 E	Consider disqualification	£90

OFFENCE	PENALTY POINTS	MAXIMUM PENALTY	COMMENTS	FINE
SEAT BELTS				
28.† Not wearing	-	Level 2		£60
29.† Driving with a child not wearing				
† (front)	-	Level 2		£60
† (back)		Level 1		£30
SPEEDING				
30.† Exceeding speed limit	3 - 6	Level 3E	Consider disqualification if 30mph over limit	SEE TABLE OF BANDS ON PAGE 50
SPEED LIMITERS				
31.† Speed Limiter not fitted	-			Driver £300 / Owner £420
32.† Speed Limiter not being used or not correctly calibrated	-			Driver £150 / Owner £210
TACHOGRAPH				
33. No tachograph or not used as required	-	Level 5		£240
34. Tachograph falsification	-	Level 5		£360
TAKEN VEHICLES				
35. ♦ Aggravated Vehicle Taking	(3-11)	Level 5 must disqualify at least 12 months and /or 6 months prison	Refer to Guidelines: Entry point for this offence is CUSTODY	
36. ♦ Taking vehicle without consent	-	Level 5 may disqualify only and/or 6 months prison	Refer to Guidelines: Entry point for this offence is COMMUNITY PENALTY	
37. Carried in taken vehicle	-	Level 5 may disqualify only and/or 6 months prison	Consider custody/community penalty	£300
TEST CERTIFICATE				
38. No test certificate	-	Level 3 but for goods vehicles and vehicles adapted to carry more than 8 passengers Level 4		Ordinary vehicles £90 / 3.5 tonnes or over GVW £120 / LGV and PCV £180 / Trailers (but dependent on size) £90
TRAFFIC LIGHTS				
39.† Failing to comply with	3	Level 3 E		£90
TRAFFIC OR POLICE SIGNS				
40.† Failing to comply with (except traffic lights or double white lines)	3	Level 3 (power to disqualify, endorse, test in some cases)	Endorse where required	£90
VEHICLE OFFENCES under the Construction and Use Regulations not shown elsewhere				
41.† Loss of wheel	3	Level 4 E but for goods vehicles etc Level 5	In all cases consider degree of responsibility	Driver £420 / Owner £800
42.† Exhaust emission	-	Level 3 but for goods vehicles etc Level 4	In all cases consider degree of responsibility	Driver £90 / Owner £150
42.† Other offences	-	Level 3 but for goods vehicles etc Level 4	In all cases consider degree of responsibility	Driver £60 / Owner £90

MOTORWAY OFFENCES

OFFENCE	PENALTY POINTS	MAXIMUM PENALTY	COMMENTS	FINE
DRIVING				
44.† Driving in reverse	3	Level 4 E	On main motorway / On sliproad	£360 / £120
45.† Driving in wrong direction	3	Level 4 E	Consider disqualification — On main motorway / On sliproad	£800 / £180
46.† Driving off carriageway	3	Level 4 E	Central reservation / Hard shoulder	£180 / £150
47.† Driving on sliproad against 'No entry sign'	3	Level 4 E		£180
48.† Making U-Turn	3	Level 4 E	Consider disqualification	£480
LEARNERS				
49.† Learner driver or excluded vehicle	3	Level 4 E		£180
SPEEDING				
50.† Exceeding speed limit	3 - 6	Level 4 E*	Consider disqualification if 30mph over limit	SEE TABLE OF BANDS BELOW

*Level 3E in respect of goods and other vehicles restricted to a lower limit

OFFENCE	PENALTY POINTS	MAXIMUM PENALTY	COMMENTS	FINE
STOPPING				
51.† Stopping on hard shoulder	-	Level 4	On main motorway / On sliproad	£120 / £60
THIRD LANE				
52.† Vehicle over 7.5 tonnes or drawing trailer in third lane	3	Level 4 E		£300
WALKING				
53.† Walking on motorway	-	Level 4	On main motorway or sliproad / On hard shoulder or verge	£90 / £60

†SPEEDING - TABLE OF BANDS

Penalty Points: 3 - 6

Maximum penalty: see numbers 30 & 50 above

Guideline for speeding, but consider scene of offence and more for heavy vehicles/LGVs/PCVs

MILES OVER LIMIT		SUGGESTED VARIABLE PENALTY POINTS	SUGGESTED FINE
1 - 14	A fixed penalty will often have been offered	3	£90
15 - 19	A fixed penalty will often have been offered	4	£120
20 - 24	A fixed penalty will often have been offered	5	£150
25 - 29	A fixed penalty may have been offered	6	£180
30 - 34	Equivalent to 100mph on the motorway - Consider disqualification	6	Disqualify for 7 days £210
35 - 39		6	Disqualify for 14 days £240

Above this speed - 40 miles or more over the limit (eg 70 mph in a 30 mph area - 110 mph on the motorway - sharp increase in penalty and disqualification (minimum 21 days).

The legal limits are:

Breath: 35 micrograms per 100 millilitres

Blood: 80 milligrams per 100 millilitres

Urine: 107 milligrams per 100 millilitres

Between 40 and 52 micrograms per 100 millilitres of breath the suggested fine is £480 and disqualification for 12 months. For amounts in excess of 52 micrograms (breath) or 120 milligrams (blood) or 160 milligrams (urine) then refer to the chart below and read off a datum or entry point for your deliberations.

For breath: take the reading on the left hand side of the chart and go to the diagonal line. Where the reading meets the diagonal, drop vertically to the base line and read off the associated fine and disqualification.

For blood: above 210, go to the right of the diagonal, drop vertically and read off fine and disqualification. Below 210, go left and proceed as above.

For urine: take the reading on the right hand side of the chart and go left to the diagonal line. Where the reading meets the diagonal, drop vertically to the base line and read off fine and disqualification.

IMPORTANT: This only provides a starting point. Always apply circumstances to increase or decrease fine or disqualification.

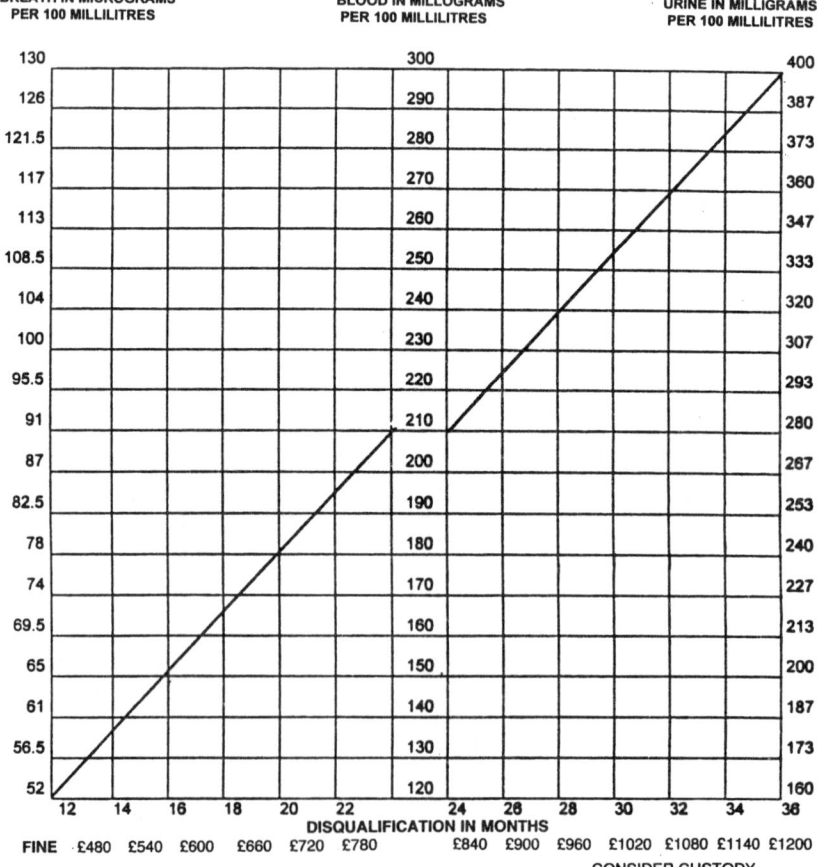

BREATH IN MICROGRAMS PER 100 MILLILITRES   BLOOD IN MILLOGRAMS PER 100 MILLILITRES   URINE IN MILLIGRAMS PER 100 MILLILITRES

DISQUALIFICATION IN MONTHS

FINE £480 £540 £600 £660 £720 £780 £840 £900 £960 £1020 £1080 £1140 £1200

-------- CONSIDER CUSTODY --------

REFUSING BREATH BLOOD OR URINE SPECIMENS (DRIVING ETC.) - £720 AND DISQUALIFY 18 MONTHS

Originated by Captain ARF Thompson DFC JP (Lymington PSD, Hampshire)

Vehicle Interference

Criminal Attempts Act 1981 s. 9
Triable only summarily
Penalty: Level 4 and/or 3 months

ENTRY POINT ↗	COMMUNITY PENALTY

CONSIDER THE SERIOUSNESS OF THE OFFENCE

eg.

eg.
- Offence committed on bail
- Group action
- Planned
- Related Damage
- Previous convictions and failures to respond to previous sentences, if relevant

IS IT SERIOUS ENOUGH FOR A COMMUNITY PENALTY?
IS COMPENSATION, DISCHARGE OR FINE APPROPRIATE, OR
IS IT SO SERIOUS THAT ONLY CUSTODY IS APPROPRIATE?

CONSIDER OFFENDER MITIGATION

eg.
- Guilty plea: *for a timely guilty plea allow a discount of about a third*
- Age, health (physical or mental)
- Co-operation with the police
- Voluntary Compensation
- Remorse

DECIDE YOUR SENTENCE

Compare your decision with the entry point - COMMUNITY PENALTY - and check your reasons if you have reached a different sentence

The court should have regard to the cost of the loss of the no claims bonus, the repairs not claimed on insurance and the loss of use of vehicle whilst being repaired

NB. COMPENSATION - Give reasons if not awarding compensation
NB. FINES - If imposing a fine, remember to increase or decrease the amount according to the financial circumstances of the offender

The Magistrates' Association

Issue March 1995

Going equipped for theft etc.

Theft Act s.25
Triable either way - see Mode of Trial Guidelines
Penalty: Level 5 and/or 6 months
May disqualify where committed with reference to the theft or taking of motor vehicles

ENTRY POINT ↗	COMMUNITY PENALTY

CONSIDER THE SERIOUSNESS OF THE OFFENCE

eg.

eg.
- Offence committed on bail
- Premeditated
- Group action
- Sophisticated
- Specialised equipment
- Number of items
- People put in fear
- Previous convictions and failures to respond to previous sentences, if relevant

IS IT SERIOUS ENOUGH FOR A COMMUNITY PENALTY?
IS COMPENSATION, DISCHARGE OR FINE APPROPRIATE, OR
IS IT SO SERIOUS THAT ONLY CUSTODY IS APPROPRIATE?

CONSIDER OFFENDER MITIGATION

eg.
- Guilty plea: *for a timely guilty plea allow a discount of about a third*
- Age, health (physical or mental)
- Co-operation with the police
- Remorse

DECIDE YOUR SENTENCE

Compare your decision with the entry point - COMMUNITY PENALTY - and check your reasons if you have reached a different sentence

Consider forfeiture of all equipment

Consider disqualification where committed with reference to the theft or taking of motor vehicles

NB. FINES - If imposing a fine, remember to increase or decrease the amount according to the financial circumstances of the offender

The Magistrates' Association

Issue June 1994

Possessing an offensive weapon

Prevention of Crime Act 1953 s.1
Triable either way - see Mode of Trial Guidelines
Penalty: Level 5 and/or 6 months

ENTRY POINT ✓   CUSTODY

⊕ CONSIDER THE SERIOUSNESS OF THE OFFENCE

eg.
Offence committed on bail
Busy public place
Group action or joint possession
People put in fear
Premeditated
Previous convictions and failures to respond
to previous sentences, if relevant

eg.
Acting out of genuine fear
Not premeditated

Consider the nature of the weapon - is it a weapon per se (consult the clerk).

IS IT SO SERIOUS THAT ONLY CUSTODY IS APPROPRIATE?
IS IT SERIOUS ENOUGH FOR A COMMUNITY PENALTY?
IS COMPENSATION, DISCHARGE OR FINE APPROPRIATE?

CONSIDER OFFENDER MITIGATION

eg.
Guilty plea: *for a timely guilty plea allow a discount of about a third*
Age, health (physical or mental)
Co-operation with the police
Remorse

DECIDE YOUR SENTENCE

Compare your decision with the entry point - CUSTODY - and check your reasons if you have
reached a different sentence

Consider forfeiture of the weapon

NB. FINES - If imposing a fine, remember to increase or decrease the amount according to the
financial circumstances of the offender

Fraudulent use etc. Vehicle Excise Licence etc.

Vehicle Excise and Registration Act 1944 s.44
Triable either way - see Mode of Trial Guidelines
Penalty: Level 5

ENTRY POINT ✓   FINE

CONSIDER THE SERIOUSNESS OF THE OFFENCE

eg.
Offence committed on bail
Deliberately planned
Disc forged or altered
Long term defrauding
LGV, HGV, PCV PSV, taxi or private hire
vehicle
Previous convictions and failures to respond
to previous sentences, if relevant

eg.
Impulsive action

IS COMPENSATION, DISCHARGE OR FINE APPROPRIATE?
IS IT SERIOUS ENOUGH FOR A COMMUNITY PENALTY?
(PROBATION IS THE ONLY AVAILABLE COMMUNITY PENALTY FOR THIS OFFENCE)

CONSIDER OFFENDER MITIGATION

eg.
Guilty plea: *for a timely guilty plea allow a discount of about a third*
Age, health (physical or mental)
Co-operation with the police
Remorse

DECIDE YOUR SENTENCE

Compare your decision with the entry point - FINE - and check your reasons if you have
reached a different sentence

Guideline fine for this offence is £240 which reflects the average seriousness of an offence of
this type for a private motor vehicle

NB. FINES - If imposing a fine, remember to increase or decrease the amount according to the
financial circumstances of the offender

Appendix C Penalty Points and Disqualification

Offence codes—endorsements and disqualification

Where a court orders a driving licence to be endorsed and/or an offender to be disqualified the details of the offences are coded. The codes appear on driving licences and DVLA printouts: see, generally, *Chapter 7*. The codes are normally abbreviations of the names of offences, eg SP = speeding, CD = careless driving. The full list of offence codes (September 1995) is as follows:

CODE	OFFENCE	POINTS

OFFENCES IN RELATION TO ACCIDENTS

AC10	Failing to stop after an accident	5-10
AC20	Failing to give particulars or to report an accident within 24 hours	5-10
AC30	Undefined accident offence	4-9

DRIVING WHILST DISQUALIFIED

BA10	Driving while disqualified by order of the court	6
BA20	Driving while disqualified as under age	Replaced by LC20 from 1 July 1992
BA30	Attempting to drive while disqualified by order of court (England/Wales only)	6

CARELESS DRIVING OFFENCES

CD10	Driving without due care and attention	3-9
CD20	Driving without reasonable consideration for other road users	3-9
CD30	Driving without due care and attention or without reasonable consideration for other road users (primarily for use by Scottish courts)	3-9 3-9
CD40	Causing death by careless driving when unfit through drink	3-11*
CD50	Causing death by careless driving when unfit through drugs	3-11*
CD60	Causing death by careless driving with alcohol level above the limit	3-11*
CD70	Causing death by careless driving then failing to provide specimen for analysis	3-11*

CONSTRUCTION AND USE OFFENCES (VEHICLES OR PARTS)

Code	Offence	Points
CU10	Using a vehicle with defective brakes	3
CU20	Causing or likely to cause danger by reason or use of unsuitable vehicle or using a vehicle with parts or accessories (excluding brakes, steering or tyres) in dangerous conditions	3
CU30	Using a vehicle with defective tyres	3
CU40	Using a vehicle with defective steering	3
CU50	Causing or likely to cause danger by reason of load or passengers	) Rescinded
CU60	Undefined failure to comply with construction and use regulation	) 1/7/92

DANGEROUS (FORMERLY RECKLESS) DRIVING OFFENCES

Code	Offence	Points
DD30	Reckless driving	Replaced by DD 40 from 1/7/92
DD40	Dangerous driving	3-11*
DD60	Manslaughter or, in Scotland, culpable homicide while driving a motor vehicle	3-11*
DD70	Causing death by reckless driving	Replaced by DD80 from 1/7/92
DD80	Causing death by dangerous driving	3-11*

DRINK OR DRUGS OFFENCES

Code	Offence	Points
DR10	Driving or attempting to drive with alcohol concentration above limit	3-11*
DR20	Driving or attempting to drive when unfit through drink	3-11*
DR30	Driving or attempting to drive then refusing to provide specimen for analysis	3-11*
DR40	In charge of a vehicle with alcohol concentration above limit	10
DR50	In charge of a vehicle when unfit through drink	10
DR60	Failure to provide a specimen for analysis in circumstances other than driving or attempting to drive	10
DR70	Failing to provide specimen for breath test	4
DR80	Driving or attempting to drive when unfit through drugs	3-11*
DR90	In charge of a vehicle when unfit through drugs	10

INSURANCE OFFENCES

IN10	Using a vehicle uninsured against third party risks	6-8

LICENCE OFFENCES

LC10	Driving without a licence	Replaced by LC20 from 1/7/92
LC20	Driving otherwise than in accordance with a licence	3-6
LC30	Driving after making a false declaration about fitness when applying for a licence	3-6
LC40	Driving a vehicle having failed to notify a disability	3-6
LC50	Driving after a licence has been revoked or refused on medical grounds	3-6

MISCELLANEOUS OFFENCES

MS10	Leaving vehicle in dangerous position	3
MS20	Unlawful pillion riding	3
MS30	Play Street offence	2
MS40	Driving with uncorrected defective eyesight or refusing to submit to a test of eyesight	3 (See MS70 and MS80)
MS50	Motor racing on the highway	3-11*
MS60	Offences not covered by other codes as appropriate	
MS70	Driving with uncorrected defective eyesight	3
MS80	Refusing to submit to an eyesight test	3
MS90	Failure to give information as to identity of driver in certain cases	3

MOTORWAY OFFENCES

MW10	Contravention of special roads regulations (excluding speed limits)	3

PEDESTRIAN CROSSING OFFENCES

PC10	Undefined contravention of pedestrian crossing regulations (primarily for use by Scottish courts)	3

Code	Offence	Points
PC20	Contravention of pedestrian crossing regulations with moving vehicles	3
PC30	Contravention of pedestrian crossing regulations with stationary vehicle	3

PROVISIONAL LICENCE OFFENCES

Code	Offence	
PL10	Driving without L-plates	)
PL20	Not accompanied by a qualified person	)
PL30	Carrying a person not qualified	) Replaced by
PL40	Drawing an unauthorised trailer	) LC 20
PL50	Undefined failure to comply with the conditions of a provisional licence	) from 1/7/92

SPEED LIMITS OFFENCES

Code	Offence	Points
SP10	Exceeding goods vehicle speed limit	3-6
SP20	Exceeding speed limit for type of vehicle (excluding goods/passenger vehicles)	3-6
SP30	Exceeding statutory speed limit on a public road	3-6
SP40	Exceeding passenger vehicle speed limit	3-6
SP50	Exceeding speed limit on a motorway	3-6
SP60	Undefined speed limit offence	3-6

TRAFFIC DIRECTIONS AND SIGNS OFFENCES

Code	Offence	Points
TS10	Failing to comply with traffic light signals	3
TS20	Failing to comply with double white lines	3
TS30	Failing to comply with a 'stop' sign	3
TS40	Failing to comply with directions of a constable or traffic warden	3
TS50	Failing to comply with a traffic sign (excluding stop signs, traffic lights or double white lines)	3
TS60	Failing to comply with school crossing patrol sign	3
TS70	Undefined failure to comply with a traffic direction or sign	3

OFFENCES OF THEFT OR UNAUTHORISED TAKING

UT10	Taking and driving away a vehicle without consent or an attempt there at (in England and Wales prior to Theft Act 1968 only). Driving a vehicle knowing it to have been taken without consent; allowing oneself to be carried in or on a vehicle knowing it to have been taken without consent. (primarily for use by Scottish courts)	)))) no longer) endorsable since) 1/7/92))))
UT20	Stealing or attempting to steal a vehicle	
UT30	Going equipped for stealing or taking a motor vehicle	
UT40	Taking or attempting to take a vehicle without consent. Driving or attempting to drive a vehicle knowing it to have been taken without consent.) Allowing oneself to be carried in or on a vehicle knowing it to have been taken without consent	
UT50	Aggravated taking of a vehicle	3-11*

SPECIAL CODE: TT99
Only used to indicate a disqualification under the totting-up procedures.

AIDING, ABETTING, COUNSELLING, PROCURING
Coded as above but with zero changed to 2 eg UT10 becomes UT12.

CAUSING OR PERMITTING
Coded as above but with zero changed to 4 eg PL10 becomes PL14.

INCITING
Coded as above but with zero changed to 6 eg DD30 becomes DD36.

SPECIAL CODE NE99
Used where points or disqualification still relevant but endorsement no longer applicable.

* These offences involve mandatory disqualification except where special reasons are found by the court. The offences then carry 'notional points'—on a range from 3 to 11—ie which are imposed if special reasons *are* found: see generally *Chapter 7*

Appendix D Section 95 Criminal Justice Act 1991

Section 95 of the 1991 Act deals with two aspects of criminal justice:

- the financial implications of decisions; and
- discrimination.

FINANCIAL IMPLICATIONS

Whilst the cost of sentences is not, conventionally speaking, a relevant consideration in arriving at an appropriate sentence (and it is hard to appreciate how it could become a decisive factor, given the statutory sentencing criteria: see, generally, *Chapter 2*), section 95 created a mechanism for people engaged in the administration of justice (ie including judges and magistrates) to be supplied with information about the financial implications of their decisions. Section 95 places a duty on the Home Secretary to 'publish each year such information as he considers expedient' for this purpose. The latest fully comparative figures are for 1992/3 in which weekly costs per offender were:

- local prison: £526 (£411 in 1993/4)
- young offender institution: £316 (£492 in 1993/4)
- community service order: £23
- probation order: £24
- supervision order: £27
- attendance centre: average *total cost* of order £190.

DISCRIMINATION

Magistrates have a general duty to act fairly, impartially and without bias—in accordance with the principles of 'natural justice'. Research and experience indicate that through lack of understanding people can give the impression of being discriminatory despite their best intentions or efforts. In one Court of Appeal ruling the Crown Court judge was reported to have said:

> You are four coloured men. I do not want you to think for one moment that if you were four white men standing here you would be getting a moment less by way of sentence than you in fact will get. You are being sentenced for robbery not for the colour of your skin.

Leaving aside the fact that the description 'coloured' is nowadays considered unacceptable, Lord Justice Roch said

> No doubt this was well intentioned but [the judge] should not have said it. The colour, race, or religion of defendants was wholly irrelevant because all were equal in the eyes of the law, the only exception being made in the case of a public order offence which was racially motivated.

Section 95 reinforces these common law principles by requiring the Home Secretary to publish each year such information as he considers expedient for the purposes of facilitating the performance by persons engaged in the administration of criminal justice of

> their duty to avoid discriminating against any person on the ground of race, sex or any other improper ground.

Publications stemming from this provision include *Race and Criminal Justice* (1992), *Gender and the Criminal Justice System* (1992), *Digest: Information on the Criminal Justice System in England and Wales* (1993) and *Race and the Criminal Justice System* (1994).

Various criminal justice agencies have taken steps to guard against discrimination and one aim is to put in place a system of ethnic monitoring which will make it possible to track a defendant's progress through the criminal justice process. Other initiatives include:

- The Judicial Studies Board has established an Ethnic Minorities Advisory Committee which has encouraged the development of a training pack for new lay magistrates and, in practice, the topic is now an integral feature of magistrates' training.

- The Justice' Clerks' Society has published two papers designed to promote equality: *Dealing with Disadvantage* (1993) and *Black People in Magistrates' Courts* (1995).

- The professional organizations involved in the probation service have taken steps to promote racial equality in all aspects of the service's work, including the production of policy statements and guidance. This action extends to the monitoring of PSRs.

Such initiatives are likely to increase, just as courts are expected to become increasingly aware of equally important discrimination issues such as gender, disability, language, culture or disadvantage. Knowledge of such matters and an awareness of their implications are of considerable importance to sentencers and deserve a high priority.

Appendix E Young Offenders

This handbook deals only with *adult* offenders, ie aged 18 years and over. Young people below that age ('youths') are sub-divided into

- 'children': aged 10 to 13 years inclusive; and
- 'young persons': aged 14 to 17 years inclusive

and normally appear in the youth court where they are sentenced by specially trained magistrates. They may, however, appear in the ordinary magistrates' court, most frequently:

- for remand (often a 'first remand' if no youth court is sitting)
- when jointly charged with someone aged 18 years or over
- when charged with aiding, abetting, counselling, procuring, allowing or permitting an offence alleged against a person aged 18 years or over (or vice versa, ie the adult may be the abettor)
- when charged with an offence arising out of circumstances which are the same as or connected with those giving rise to an offence with which a person aged 18 years or over is charged.

In the event of conviction, the magistrates'court must normally remit the offender to the youth court for sentence but in certain circumstances it may decide to retain jurisdiction when its sentencing powers are then restricted to:

- a discharge (absolute or conditional)
- a fine (subject to special maxima)
- binding over the parent or guardian
- a supervision order.
- any appropriate ancillary orders eg for compensation, endorsement, forfeiture.

There is merit in remitting a case to the youth court after conviction (particularly if a supervision order is in prospect) unless the outcome is clearly straightforward Among other considerations:

- youth court magistrates receive special training
- the sentencing powers of the youth court are more flexible and specifically designed for a younger age group
- the 'welfare principle' in the Children and Young Persons Act 1933—to which youth courts are attuned—is often difficult to

reconcile with the underlying 'just deserts' approach to sentencing (see, generally, *Chapter 2*). The 1933 Act states that:

> Every court in dealing with a child or young person who is brought before it, either as an offender or otherwise, shall have regard to the welfare of the child or young person, and shall in a proper case take steps for removing him from undesirable surroundings, and for securing that proper provision is made for his education and training.

• the rules for PSRs are stricter in relation to youths—meaning that in practice there will often have to be an adjournment anyway.

However, there may be occasions when jurisdiction can reasonably be retained, especially if the youth and the adult are very close in age and it is felt that one bench should sentence both. Generally speaking, legal advice is advisable due to these and other special considerations such as 'parental responsibility' for the payment of fines and compensation (which differs according to whether the youth is aged 15 or less), the practical implications of binding over a parent, or the interaction of the two jusrisdictions.

A note on supervision orders

Supervision orders may be made for up to three years. The supervisor will be a local authority social worker or a probation officer. The order may include requirements for the child or young person:

—to live at a particular place
—to attend at a specified place at specified times
—to take part in various forms of activity (including, in some instances, highly intensive programmes of supervised activities)
—to remain at home for specified periods between 6pm and 6am
—to refrain from taking part in specified activities
—to receive psychiatric treatment
—to attend school or follow other educational arrangements
—to live in local authority accommodation for a specified period of up to six months.

A note on publicity

The press is severely restricted concerning what can be reported from the *youth court*. When a youth appears in the *adult court* (in whatever capacity) that court may wish to consider discretionary restrictions: seek legal advice.

Appendix F Appeals

Anyone who has been convicted and sentenced by a magistrates' court can appeal to the Crown Court against the conviction, sentence, or both or to the High Court on a point of law. The prosecutor cannot appeal against an acquittal, or against what he or she believes to be an over-lenient sentence (a form of appeal which is currently restricted to certain sentences imposed by the Crown Court).

Appeal to the Crown Court
This is the normal method of appeal against a decision by magistrates. The convicted person must give notice of appeal within 21 days of being sentenced. This can be extended by the Crown Court (called 'leave to appeal out of time'). The notice of appeal must set out the details of the conviction and sentence and state the grounds of appeal.

* *Appeal against conviction*
Appeals against conviction are heard by a Judge sitting with two magistrates (usually: there can be up to four magistrates). There is no jury. The case is heard afresh. The Crown Court either upholds the conviction or substitutes an acquittal. If the Crown Court convicts the accused it then proceeds to sentence.

* *Appeal against sentence*
Similarly, an appeal against sentence is heard by a Judge and two magistrates. The court is addressed by the appellant (ie the person making the appeal) or his or her legal representative. The Crown Court can confirm the decision or substitute its own sentence, either a more severe or lesser one—but limited to magistrates' maximum powers of punishment as described in this handbook.

Appeal to the Divisional Court
Appeals on points of law go to the Queen's Bench Division of the High Court of Justice (QBD)—where they are heard by a 'Divisional Court' of the QBD. There are three methods:

* *Case stated*
Here, the magistrates state a case for the opinion of the High Court. This involves setting down in writing what facts the magistrates found to exist in the case and then saying what law or legal principles they applied to those facts. The Divisional

Court either upholds the magistrates' decision or makes some other order, eg quashing the conviction; or ordering the magistrates to rehear the case applying the law correctly. There is a timetable for the various stages. The process starts with an application by *either* party for the magistrates to state a case for the opinion of the High Court—which must be made within 21 days of the final decision by the magistrates court. Magistrates can refuse a 'frivolous' application, or ask the applicant to identify the point of law involved eg where they are unable to discern a legal issue which actually bore on the decision.

• *Judicial review*
Anyone who is aggrieved by a decision of magistrates (which can extend beyond the parties themselves to other people with a legitimate interest in the outcome of the case—what is called *locus standi*) may ask the Divisional Court to review the case in order to see whether eg the court acted judicially, fairly, without bias, observing principles of natural justice, or whether it followed the correct procedures. If it did not, the remedy is one or more of the 'prerogative orders': *certiorari* to quash a decision; *mandamus* to compel the magistrates' court to act (eg by hearing the case in a proper manner); and *prohibition* to prevent magistrates acting in error. Judicial review must normally be pursued within six months.

• *Declarations*
More rare, are applications to the Divisional Court by either party for that court merely to declare what the law is on a particular point, or what it means. The magistrates' court then acts on the advice given.

Rectification of mistakes
Magistrates' court have power to correct their own mistakes in certain circumstances: seek legal advice.

Free pardon
Free pardons are awarded by the Sovereign. This might occur, eg where the normal appeal mechanisms are exhausted, or they cannot be used for some reason eg because the time limit for an appeal has expired but facts affecting conviction or sentence have only just surfaced. A pardon does not remove a conviction; but it erases the consequences.

157

Index

Further reading:

Introduction to the
Magistrates' Court
Bryan Gibson
SECOND EDITION

An ideal introduction. Includes a unique *Glossary of Words, Phrases and Abbreviations* containing 750 items. ISBN 1 872 870 15 5. Price £10 plus £1.50 postage and packing.

Introduction to the
Criminal Justice Process
Bryan Gibson
Paul Cavadino

The process of investigation, arrest, prosecution, trial and sentence with cameos of each of the main participants. The first book to treat the subject in this easy to read way. ISBN 1 872 870 09 0. Price £12 plus £1.50 postage and packing.

Introduction to the
Probation Service
Anthony Osler

A highly readable account of the work of the Probation Service of England and Wales. ISBN 1 872 870 19 8. Price £10 plus £1.50 postage and packing.

⌐he direct mail price appears ⌐inst each book title. Please add ⌐ per book p&p to a maximum ⌐UK only. Postage abroad is at cost).

When these three introductory titles are ordered for delivery together the total cost is £32 inclusive (saving £4.50 p&p: UK only)

Please send your order to WATERSIDE PRESS, Domum Road, Winchester S023 9NN. Telephone or Fax 01962 855567. Cheques should be made out to 'Waterside Press'. Organizations can be invoiced for two or more books on request.

Please contact Waterside Press for:

* *a full list of current and forthcoming titles*

* *details of our CRIMINAL POLICY SERIES under the editorship of Professor Andrew Rutherford.*

General interest:

Relational Justice
Edited by Jonathan Burnside and Nicola Baker. Foreword by Lord Woolf. 'Relationships as a reform dynamic for criminal justice'. ISBN 1 872 870 22 8. Price £10 plus £1.50 postage and packing

Criminal Classes
Angela Devlin. An examination of the links between educational failure and future offending behaviour. ISBN 1 872 870 30 9. Price £16 plus £1.50 postage and packing.